ART BOOKS

FROM CRESCENT MOON PUBLISHING

Leonardo da Vinci
by James Pearson

Early Netherlandish Painting
by Rosalind Mutter

Piero della Francesca
by Naomi Haskell

Giovanni Bellini
by Julia Davis

Eric Gill: Nuptials of God
by Anthony Hoyland

Minimal Art and Artists In the 1960s and After
by Laura Garrard

Postwar Art
by George Knighton

Vincent van Gogh: Visionary Landscapes
by Stuart Morris

Max Beckmann
by Stuart Morris

Egon Schiele: Sex and Death in Purple Stockings
by D. Simon Eade

Mark Rothko: The Art of Transcendence
by Julia Davis

Jasper Johns
by L.M. Poole

Brice Marden
by Laura Garrard

Frank Stella: American Abstract Artist
by James Pearson

The Light Eternal: J.M.W. Turner
by Jeremy Mark Robinson

Maurice Sendak and the Art of Children's Book Illustration
by L.M. Poole

Sex in Art: Pornography and Pleasure in Painting and Sculpture
by Cassidy Hughes

*Glorification: Religious Abstraction
In Renaissance and 20th Century Painting*
by Jeremy Mark Robinson

The Art of Andy Goldsworthy
by William Malpas

Andy Goldsworthy: Touching Nature
by William Malpas

Andy Goldsworthy In Close-Up
by William Malpas

The Art of Richard Long
by William Malpas

Constantin Brancusi: Sculpting the Essence of Things
by James Pearson

Alison Wilding: The Embrace of Sculpture
by Susan Quinnell

*The Erotic Object: Sexuality in Sculpture
From Prehistory to the Present Day*
by Susan Quinnell

*Land Art: A Complete Guide to Landscape, Environmental,
Earthworks, Nature, Sculpture and Installation Art*
by William Malpas

Land Art In Close-Up
by William Malpas

*Colourfield Painting: Minimal, Cool, Hard Edge, Serial
and Post-Painterly Abstract Art From the Sixties to the Present*
by Laura Garrard

GOYA

GOYA

BY FRANCOIS CRASTRE

TRANSLATED FROM THE FRENCH
BY FREDERIC TABER COOPER

CRESCENT MOON

First published 1914. This edition © 2017.

Printed and bound in the U.S.A.
Set in Book Antiqua 10 on 14pt.
Designed by Radiance Graphics.

British Library Cataloguing in Publication data

ISBN-13 9781861716248 (Pbk)
ISBN-13 9781861717184 (Hbk)

CRESCENT MOON PUBLISHING
P.O. Box 1312, Maidstone, Kent, ME14 5XU
Great Britain, www.crmoon.com

CONTENTS

Note On the Text   9

Goya   15

The Youth of Goya   19

The Glorious Period   51

The Closing Years   62

Notes On the Works   84

NOTE ON THE TEXT

The text is from *Goya* by Francois Crastre, translated by
Frederic Taber Cooper, and published by Frederick A. Stokes
Company, New York, 1914.

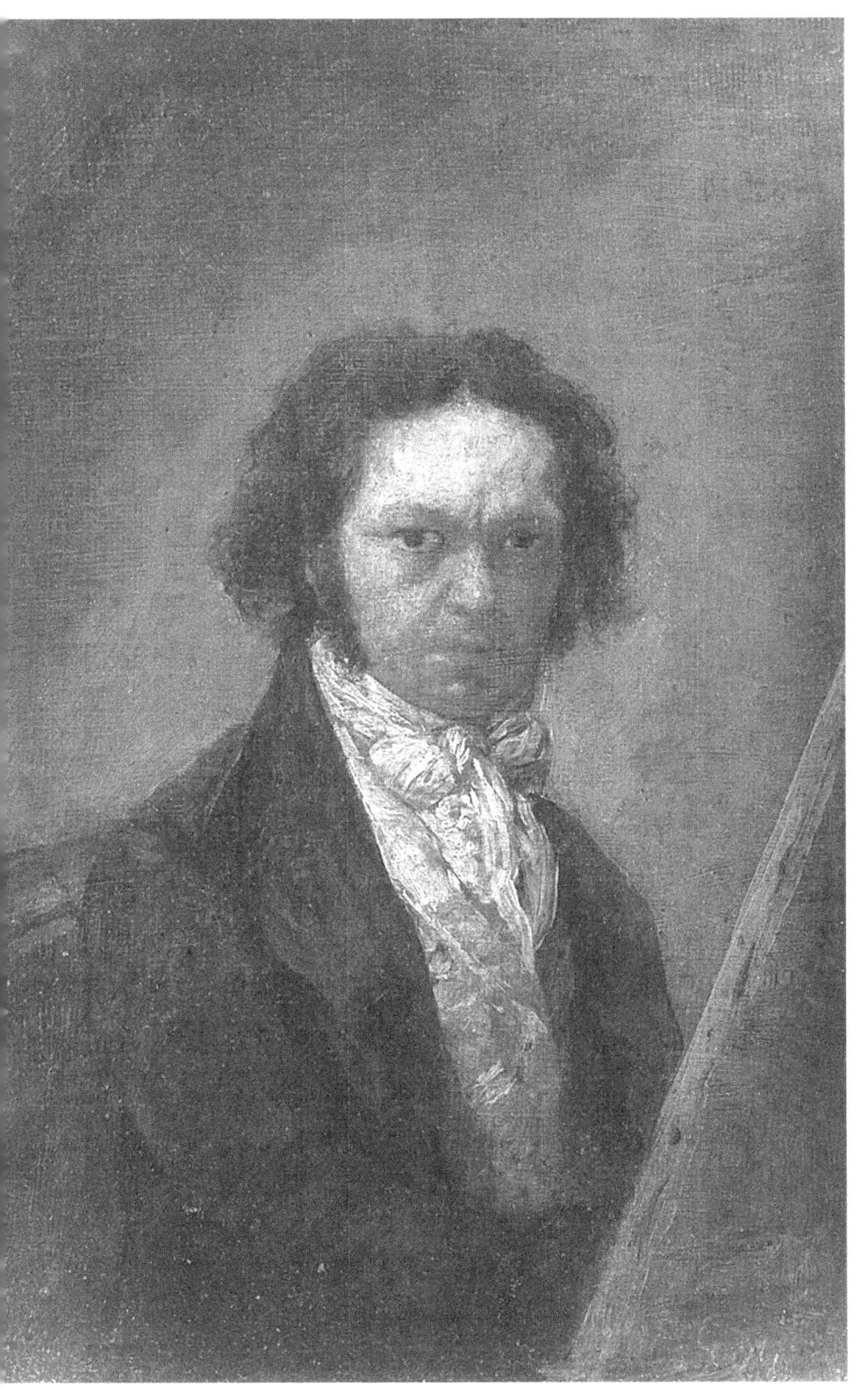

Francisco Goya, Self-Portrait, 1795, Madrid

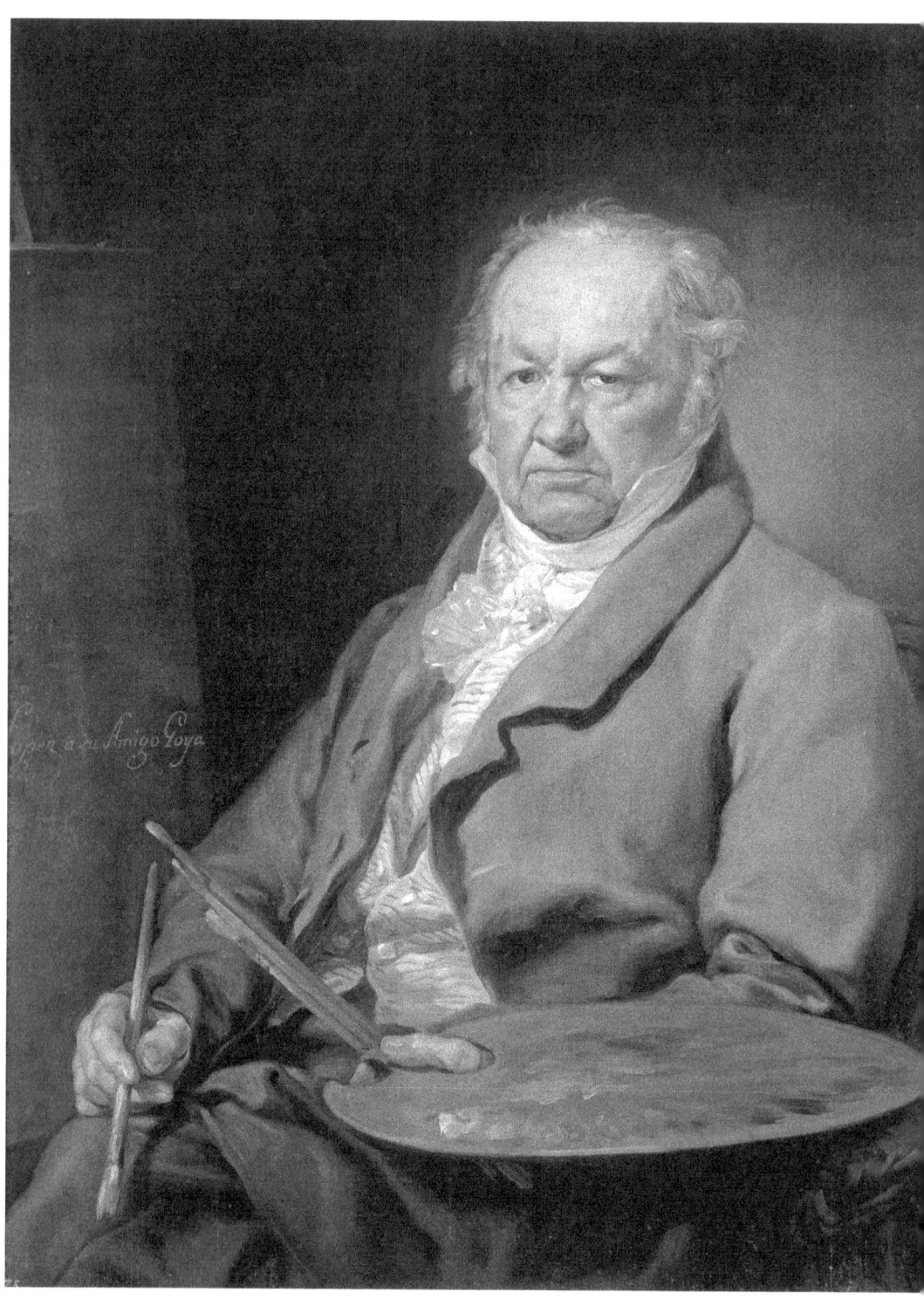

Vicente López, Portrait of Francisco de Goya, 1826, Madrid

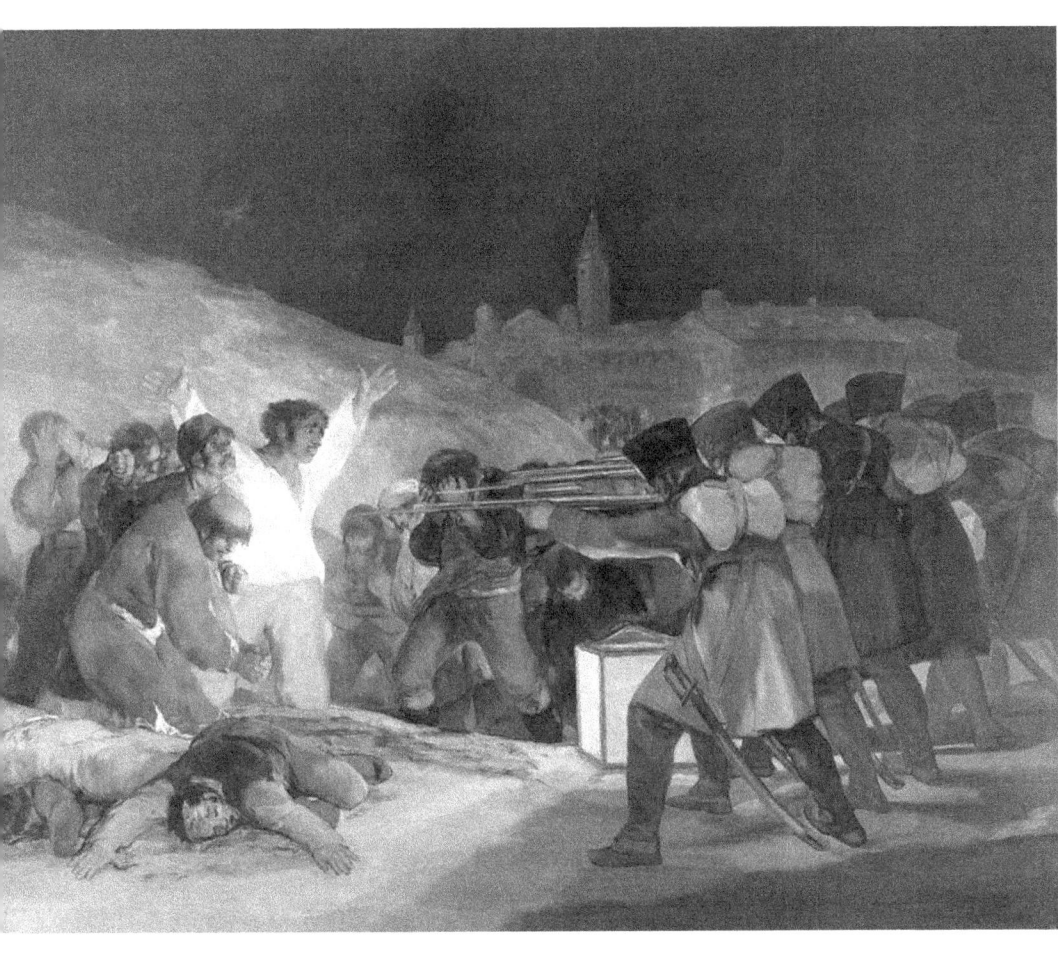

Francisco Goya, El Tres de Mayo, 1814, Prado, Madrid

On a certain clear morning in the year 1760, a monk from the convent of Santa Fé, near Saragossa, was proceeding leisurely along the road which leads to that city, and reciting his breviary as he went. Raising his eyes from between two psalms, he perceived a young lad of some fifteen years of age deeply absorbed in drawing pictures with a bit of charcoal on one of the walls which bounded the way. The monk was a lover of the arts and had himself some little skill in drawing. Becoming interested, he drew nearer, and was amazed at the aptitude shown by the boy. Upon questioning him, he was much pleased with his replies and was completely won by his engaging manners. Without further reflection, he inquired the way to the home of the lad's parents, poor peasants of the immediate neighbourhood, and had no difficulty in persuading them to entrust their son to him, promising to make him a painter of whom they would some day be proud.

History has not preserved the name of the worthy monk so kindly disposed to art, but the boy was destined to make his own name illustrious: Francisco José Goya y Lucientes, the poor son of farming folk of Saragossa, fulfilled the promises of his patron. He had talent; better yet, he had genius; he fraternized with princes and with kings, and the renown of his glory restored its lost dignity to the art of Spain and did honour to painting throughout the world.

The advent of Goya in the middle of the eighteenth century marks a sort of providential date in the art of the peninsula. The Spanish school had fallen into profound decadence. Of the great traditions of Velazquez, Ribera, Zurbaran, and El Greco, nothing survived save the regret of knowing that they were forever lost. All the prodigious strength and powerful realism of that glorious period had become degenerate, enfeebled, anaemic to the point of utter decrepitude. In the horde of artists of that time, not a single hand was capable of taking up the brush let fall by the great predecessors. One only in all their number, a certain Claudio Coello, mustered sufficient energy to attempt to carry on the broken tradition. With praiseworthy insistence and undoubted talent he endeavoured to restore its bygone dignity to the painting of his time. Among many other noteworthy works, a magnificent canvas from his hand may still be seen in the sacristy of the Escurial. But this unlucky artist, like all the others, had come too late into a world which had grown too old. He could no longer be understood. The same decadence had overspread the whole of Europe, but to a greater degree in Spain than elsewhere. Politics, customs, traditions, popular taste, all bore the imprint of that degeneracy which heralds the end of a race. What could a Claudio Coello do in a society that had disintegrated to such a degree? His strength seemed too brutal, his realism was accused of barbarity, and the conscientiousness of his line-work caused him to be considered as a painter who had become old-fashioned and had fallen behind his times. All the favour of that period was bestowed upon the *fa presto* school of painting. Luca Giordano, who usurped Coello's place in the regard of Philip II., had begun to inundate Spain with his facile and spiritless productions. He covered the walls of the Escurial with frescoes brushed in with a turn of the wrist, the dexterity of which ill concealed their absolute lack of inspiration. In his wake a swarm of Neapolitan painters, equally dexterous, but of even less worth, swooped down upon the peninsula, and day by day still further perverted the standard of popular taste. With the dawn of the seventeenth century the decadence, instead of diminishing, became more accentuated. The Neapolitans had been succeeded by Frenchmen – but what Frenchmen! Their art had neither the nobility of Poussin, nor the greatness of Le Brun, nor the suavity of Le Sueur; they bore such names as Ranc, Hovasse, Louis and Michel Vanloo, and their manner drew its inspiration from the worst type of composition brought into fashion by Mignard. Their whole effort was confined to producing the merely pretty, and their tastelessness was absolutely, yet regrettably, adapted to the growing affectation of the century. After them came the turn of the Tiepolos: these latter were not merely remarkable virtuosos of the palette; their prodigious facility was frequently ennobled by genuine talent; their line-work, though too often slighted, still showed a certain degree of conscientiousness, and some of their works are really worthy of admiration. But they too were infected with the malady of the century; they sacrificed themselves to the taste of their day, which was definitely degraded to the extravagances of fashion and the frivolities of gallantry. They were wholly lacking in the ability to impart to this type of painting the vivacious charm which the graceful and smiling ease of Watteau, Fragonard, and Boucher bestowed upon it in France. There was no ground for hoping that they would ever effect a renaissance of the Spanish school.

Finally Charles III. summoned to Madrid a painter of German origin, Mengs by name, who at that time was regarded as the Messiah of an art which was destined to unite "the grace of Apelles, the expression of Raphael, the chiaroscuro of Correggio, and the colouring of Titian!" Unusually gifted though he was, Mengs did not possess the necessary calibre to fulfil such brilliant promises. Haunted by the great compositions of Le Brun, he confined himself to the mythological order of painting and drew his inspiration from his illustrious model, without ever achieving an equal eminence or duplicating the latter's admirable skill in composition. Upon his appointment as Superintendent of Fine-Arts in Spain, he established a sort of artistic dictatorship, which forced Spanish painting as a whole to adopt his own special aesthetic creed. The influence of Mengs would have been even more disastrous than that of his predecessors, if Providence had not placed Goya in the path of the artist monk of Saragossa.

Goya made his appearance, and with him Spanish art underwent a renewal and an aggrandizement. With one formidable backward leap, he attained the point of the broken tradition, in order to reweld the glorious chain. No intermediary connects him with the splendid lineage of Spanish painters. He proceeds directly from them. He is the natural heir of Velazquez and Zurbaran. He has their ardour, their vehemence, their passionate love for nature; like them, he finds the source of his strength in direct observation; as with them, the secret of his genius resides in that inner flame which bursts out of bounds in blazing flashes, with no clever trickery, no premeditation, but with that spontaneity which is born only of a clear vision, aided by a vigorous brush.

Nevertheless, this descendant of bygone masters is the most modern of all Spanish painters. He is never imitative, he always creates. From the living springs of great art he draws only what he needs to sustain his strength: a pious reverence for form, conscientiousness in line-work, sobriety of colour, and harmony of the component parts. For the rest, he is wholly of his own time, and of none other than his own time. He is truly the painter of national Spanish life. What he paints most willingly, most gladly, are the dances, the games, the joyous gatherings, the *corridas*, full of ardour and of movement, the *majas*, the *manolas*, the *toreros*, all the popular types; and one and all, as he pictures them, are spirited, life-like, entertaining, and well grouped, standing out boldly against their background of spreading fields, or bathing gaily in the violent clarity of the sunshine of Castile.

When considered under this double aspect, surrounded by the twin aureole of classicism and realism, Goya is seen to be an exceptional nature. He builds his fantasies upon a solid foundation of technique, and it is precisely because he founds his work upon this impregnable basis that he is able without apprehension to challenge the judgment of future centuries, and that his name will descend through the ages crowned with an unfading glory.

HIS YOUTH

Francisco José Goya was born at Fuendetodos, in the province of Aragon, on the 13th of March, 1746. His father, José Goya, and his mother, Gracia Lucientes, were humble peasants and lived upon the product of the sluggish fields that surrounded their modest home. What the childhood of José was, we do not know, for his biographers are silent upon this point. They content themselves with saying that he aided his parents in the daily round of tasks upon the farm. As to his education, it was certainly that of all the young peasant boys of the Spanish farming districts. The child must have acquired the first rudiments from the village priest, or perhaps from the monks of the nearest convent. Reading, writing, and a little arithmetic made up the whole equipment that young José possessed at the age of fifteen. How his taste for drawing was first born, what occurrence or what object awakened his artistic instinct, we do not know. Perhaps, like so many others, he became suddenly conscious of his vocation at the sight of some of those cruel and violent pictures representing scenes of the Passion, such as abound in Spanish churches, and it is not unlikely that his youthful soul received a profound and lasting impression.

However this may be, at the age of fifteen Goya could handle his pencil with sufficient assurance to astonish the worthy monk of Saragossa, who was a judge of such matters. The latter conducted his young protégé to the city, and a few days later entered him as a pupil in the studio of Don José Lujan Martinez.

This Lujan was a Saragossan by birth, but he had studied painting in Naples under the guidance of Mastréolo. Possessing considerable talent, he enjoyed a great reputation in his native city. Upon his return from Italy, he had founded a free school of design, a sort of academy which was maintained wholly by his own contributions, both of money and of time.

Among the artists who were trained in this studio, there were some who left names highly esteemed in Spain: Beraton, Vallespin, Antonio Martinez the goldsmith, and Francisco Bayeu de Subias. With the last named of this group Goya formed a particular attachment, notwithstanding that Bayeu was twelve years the elder.

Goya remained in Lujan's studio for between four and five years. His fiery and impulsive temperament had already begun to declare itself, and his master did not always succeed in moderating his exuberance. He manifested an extraordinary diligence in his work, he was enamoured of his art, and showed exceptional aptitude for it. From the first months he became the most interesting feature in the studio; his imagination, his enthusiasm, his assurance often surprised his master and stupefied his comrades, who were accustomed to a calmer and less violent manner of painting. At this epoch his character was already beginning to form; one could foresee in him the man that he was destined to be throughout his life. He was no less ardent in his pleasures than in his work. He was the true type of the hot-headed Aragonais, and at the age of nineteen revealed himself, headstrong, turbulent, a born fighter. He threw himself, heart and soul, into the battles that occurred so frequently at that time throughout Aragon between the young men of the different parishes. Uniting in rival gangs, fiercely jealous of one another, they were always ready on holiday evenings to settle some question of superiority, and any excuse for an encounter was welcomed by them. More than once, for the greater honour of San Luis or of Nuestra Señora del Pilar, the club and knife scattered blood over the streets and suburbs of Saragossa.

Goya took part in all these battles, flung himself into them, body and soul, tumultuously aiding and abetting this hazardous and adventurous mode of life, which had the flavour of romantic fiction. In the course of one of these collisions, three young men belonging to the rival faction were left stiff and stark on the battle-ground. Goya, who was one of those most directly implicated in the affair, was warned that the Inquisition intended to arrest him. Although it no longer possessed the terrible power of earlier times, the Inquisition was even then by no means light-handed, and there was still serious danger in bringing oneself under its notice. Goya was well aware of this, and he did not wait for the arrival of the *alguazils*. That same night he left the city and wended his way to Madrid, which, as it happened, it had long been his dream to visit.

In Madrid he once more ran across his friend Bayeu, who had been living there for the past two years. Bayeu was drawing a pension from the academy of San Fernando, and he also had the good luck of being favoured by Mengs, the all powerful Superintendent of Fine-Arts, who had asked him to collaborate in his great task of decorating the royal palace.

Bayeu welcomed his young comrade with open arms and invited him to have a share in his present work. But we must infer that Mengs's technique and method of teaching were already displeasing to Goya, for he courteously declined the offer. In any case, he had not come to Madrid in search of employment, but for the purpose of continuing his education. All day long he visited the artistic marvels of the capital, made the rounds of churches and convents, studied the old masters, executed copies, and even penetrated into the royal dwellings in order to admire the works of art which they contained, observing extensively, reflecting, comparing, and, in a word, equipping his profound intelligence with precious material for the future. But in Madrid, just as in Saragossa, work was not allowed to interfere with his pleasures. He was always to be found in quest of adventure; he roamed the streets, sword under cape and guitar in hand, serenading the sparkling black eyes that looked down laughingly at him from the ambush of their window-blinds, and stirring husbands to a jealous fury; or again, breaking the peace with a crowd of boisterous companions; or still again, scaling the balcony of his latest conquest, "and thus playing the prelude to that reputation of an audacious, swash-buckling Don Juan, which later was destined to earn him, even among the lower classes, an incredible notoriety."

At this period Goya was a young man of haughty presence, somewhat below the average stature, but exceedingly well proportioned. Although his features lacked regularity, his face was attractive. It had a pleasant air of joviality and frankness; there was a sparkle to his eye and a lurking spirit of mischief around his lips. He had, furthermore, an affable manner, an unabashed assurance, a mad bravado, and the impudence of a lackey. Thanks to the friends whom he had gained, he was favourably received by a goodly number of distinguished families, where the charm of his personality played havoc with the hearts of the women.

This agreeable pastime could not fail to entail its own dangers, as Goya was not long in learning by experience. On a certain fine evening, when he had doubtless been lurking beneath some balcony, he was picked up in an obscure side street, where he lay stretched at full length, with a gaping poignard thrust in his back. It was necessary to keep him hidden for a time, in order to protect him from the unwelcome curiosity of the police; and later, when the affair had become noised abroad, he was forced to quit Madrid, just as he had quitted Saragossa, clandestinely, without even waiting for his wound to be completely healed.

In order to give his escapade a chance to be forgotten, Goya, who for some time past had desired to visit Italy, set sail, with Rome for his destination.

From the moment of his arrival he came fully under the spell of the marvels accumulated in the Eternal City. He passed entire days in the presence of the masterpieces of the great artists. He admired them with all his heart, yet without surrendering his right to independent criticism. He recognized instinctively that there was nothing in all these illustrious compositions which corresponded to his own personal temperament, and that his fiery soul could ill adapt itself to the calculated and almost geometric composition of the great frescoes in the Vatican. But he possessed too deep a reverence for art to disdain the admirable science of those great forerunners. There, beyond question, was the ideal opportunity for study; and in the presence of those celebrated canvases he absolutely forgot himself; he analyzed their intimate beauties, compared the styles and colour schemes of the different schools, scrutinized their methods, and forced himself to penetrate and understand them. He did not attempt to copy a single one of them; he felt that he would gain nothing by doing so, but that on the contrary he might lose. This singular method of abstract study, which may be called the method of intuition, explains perhaps how so frank an individuality as that of Goya, far from being enfeebled by contact with the past, became on the contrary stronger and more genuinely alive. As a matter of fact, his talent owes nothing, or practically nothing, to the art of Italy.

During his sojourn in Rome, Goya came in contact with David. Curious phenomenon; these two natures who were so different in character and temperament, and whose artistic tastes were almost antagonistic, felt themselves invincibly attracted towards each other. It is true that they both shared to an equal degree the philosophic ideas of the period, and that they had the same ideal; namely, the liberation of the people. They were destined later, each in his own country, to be caught in the full whirlwind of the Revolution; and these mutual ties, divined rather than expressed, created between David and Goya an undying friendship. Because they liked each other, they appreciated each other's work, in spite of the divergence between their talents; and Goya, even in extreme old age, always spoke with emotion of the "great David."

In Rome, as in Madrid, Goya was not long in distinguishing himself by perilous escapades. Señor Carderera relates that at one time

> "He carved his name with his knife on the lantern of Michelangelo's cupola, on a corner of a certain stone which not one of the artists, German, English, or French, who had preceded him in the mad ascent, had succeeded in reaching; and on another day he made the circuit of the tomb of Cecilia Metella, barely supporting himself upon the narrow projection of the cornice."

But these were merely childish pranks; before long he had involved himself in a far more dangerous adventure, especially in the city of the Popes. He had become infatuated with a young girl in the higher circles of Roman society, and formed the project of eloping with her. Being warned in time, the parents placed their daughter beyond his reach, within the austere shelter of a convent. This setback, however, was not sufficient to discourage the gallant artist, it only spurred him on to bolder ventures. He resolved to snatch his fair lady from the very hands of her jailors, and one night he attempted to invade the convent itself. But he was captured and handed over to justice. In order to extricate himself from this awkward dilemma, far more awkward at Rome than it would have been anywhere else, he was forced to appeal to the Spanish ambassador, who intervened and demanded his surrender by the Holy See. Goya was restored to liberty, but on condition that he should take immediate leave of Rome.

He now returned to Saragossa, for the sake of his aged parents, with whom he spent the closing months of the year 1774, after which he once more set forth for Madrid. There he again fell in with his faithful friend, Bayeu, discovered himself to be in love with the latter's sister, Josefa Bayeu, and married her a few months later.

His brother-in-law again offered to introduce him to Mengs, and this time, weary no doubt of adventures, he accepted the offer. The Superintendent of Fine-Arts gave him a most cordial reception. We have already had occasion to refer to the almost despotic authority which Mengs at this period exerted over Spanish art and the singular direction in which he had guided it. In the decorative works which he was conducting in the palaces at Madrid and Aranjuez, there was, in the words of M. Charles Yriarte, "nothing but an agglomeration of struggles of Titans, apotheoses, triumphs of Hercules, and glorifications of Ceres; but Goya soon came to scale Olympus, and turn Venus into a manola, and substitute his frightful *Saturn devouring his Children*, in his *Quinta* [Goya's country house], for the figure of Father Time, with his traditional stooping shoulders, partaking of his progeny with prudence and circumspection."

Up to this moment Goya had been far more intent upon observing and learning than upon painting; he had as yet produced nothing, and no one even suspected the powerful faculties that were dormant in him. More as a favour to Bayeu than from any personal confidence, Mengs entrusted him with the composition of some cartoons for the royal manufactory of Santa Barbara. Goya set to work, and from the start broke squarely away from the superannuated tradition of the Superintendent. Throwing aside the entire paraphernalia of mythology, he confined his cartoons wholly to subjects borrowed from national life. In this work he gave free rein to the full spontaneity of his talent and to his riotous imagination, and in the course of it he revealed the full wealth of his imagination and his marvellous instinct for decorative art. The result was a revelation: a genuine ovation greeted these modern compositions, so full of life and movement and colour. Mengs himself, who was not lacking either in intelligence or in taste, was frankly delighted and warmly congratulated the young artist. At Court and in the city nothing was talked of but Goya and his cartoons; from this moment he entered upon his true role as national painter.

Henceforth, throughout a period of more than fifty years, he was destined to produce unweariedly, trying his hand at the most diverse types, alternating between painting and engraving; and in his life-work, which, taken as a whole, is one of the vastest and most varied that ever came from any artist, he has given us the measure of his prodigious fecundity.

He made his debut in genre painting, and he drew his inspiration straight from the life of the people. Spain, for that matter, furnished an exceptional nutriment for his order of talent; land that it was of vivid light, ardent colour, picturesque manners and curious costumes, it was well designed to fire that vigorous and impulsive nature to the highest pitch of enthusiasm. And hence, while Madrid looked on and marvelled, there came in swift succession from his brush a whole series of pictures saturated with local colour: bull fights, attacks of bandits, clandestine meetings, processions, masquerades, all the life of the Spanish city and the Spanish highway, reproduced in piquant, accurate, brightly coloured scenes, of charming naïveté and exquisite naturalness, replete with vivacity and riotous fancy.

On closer inspection it would be easy to find a certain amount of incorrectness in the drawing. Some of his bulls, especially, are endowed with anatomical proportions that at best only approximate the truth. But they have such spirit, such vigour, such nimbleness, such furious agility, that we feel ourselves snatched up and borne along by this living whirlwind, this intensity of movement, almost as though we were bodily present in the arena where the blood-stained drama is in the course of enactment. As to the colouring, it is very light and very luminous and silvery.

Almost at the same period Goya published a collection of etchings in which he had reproduced the most celebrated masterpieces of Velazquez. It was a daring venture, but it had no terrors for the young artist. Goya did no injustice to Velazquez; he succeeded most felicitously in reproducing in these etchings not only the design, but the colour values and characteristic spirit of his model. This magnificent series, executed during the year 1778, comprises sixteen pieces, which to-day are of inestimable value.

That same year the Franciscans went to great expense to decorate their church; they appealed to the most renowned artists which Madrid at that period possessed. Goya was entrusted with the decoration of a chapel which required two paintings. The subjects specified were a *Christ on the Cross* and a *St. Francis Preaching*. The *Christ on the Cross* is distinguished by a very fine religious spirit, enhanced by its admirable drawing and by a dignity quite its own. The fine and delicate modelling suggests comparison with the most perfect works of Italy; and the whole painting is overspread with an infinitely light surface coat of colour, very luminous and very pale.

This canvas is the best of all Goya's religious works. On the contrary, his *St. Francis Preaching* in no way deserved the vogue which it enjoyed at the time, both at Court and in the city circles. Its heavy composition, pretentious and ill balanced, did no credit to any of Goya's qualities, save that of colourist, in which respect he was always interesting.

Goya was now the idol of the whole population of Madrid, who revelled in his fantasies and regarded him as their national painter. Already celebrated through his scenes of the life of the people, he had now acquired a new prestige through the fame of his religious paintings; and there was good reason for astonishment that he had not yet been rewarded by any official honour. His rival painters had scant love for him, or, to put it more frankly, they hated the powerful originality of his talent so far removed from the slow product of their uninspired toil. In order to belittle him, they censured the incorrectness of his drawing and the violent character of his subjects. But public opinion triumphed over this dead weight of malevolence. However reluctantly, the Academy of Saint-Marc welcomed him among its members on the seventh of May, 1780, hailing him as "academician by merit."

A few months later the Chapter of Nuestra Señora del Pilar at Saragossa decided to have its sanctuary decorated and instituted a competition among the leading artists of Spain, under the direction of Goya's brother-in-law, Francisco Bayeu. Goya decided to compete, and one of the vaults, with its adjacent panels, was assigned to him. The sketches which he submitted were only half satisfactory, and the Chapter requested him to modify them. Goya took the criticisms in ill part, imputing them, whether rightly or wrongly, to his brother-in-law's jealousy, and refused in any way to modify his designs. A bitter quarrel might have resulted, if mutual friends had not intervened to reconcile the two artists. Finally, Goya agreed to make certain concessions; the vault was entrusted to him, and he forthwith commenced the execution of his frescoes.

The subject chosen represented *The Virgin and the Martyred Saints in their Glory.* This immense work required no less than three years of the artist's time, and he expended upon it all his science and all his exceptional qualities as a colourist. It is an attractive work, cleverly composed, possessing a fine decorative effect, brilliant and warm, and in no way inferior to the most resplendent frescoes of Tiepolo. Only one thing was lacking, the religious spirit, of which Goya was wholly destitute. In works of this order, dexterity is not sufficient; the breath of the inner zeal is necessary; cleverness, dexterity, the gift of colour, cannot make up for the absence of faith. As often as Goya attempted religious painting, the result showed the same general order of deficiencies, because he always treated his subjects solely as a painter, and not, after the manner of Raphael and Correggio, as a devout believer.

Furthermore, the ideal was not in his line; the dominant note of his talent, before all else, was naturalism. Genre painter by temperament, he sought by preference for the picturesque aspect of his subjects. Owing to these conditions, his frescoes at Saragossa and in general all his large religious compositions are in reality nothing else than vast genre paintings.

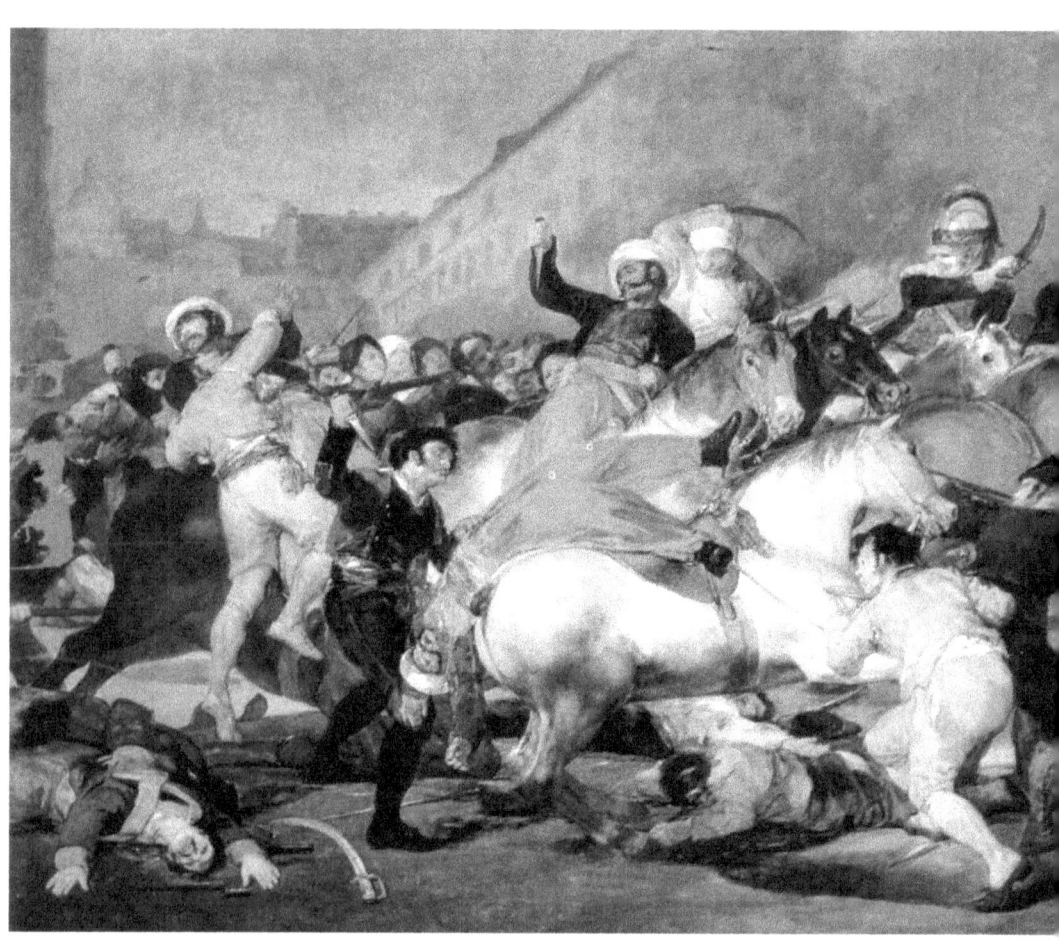

Francisco Goya, The Second of May, 1808, 1814, Madrid

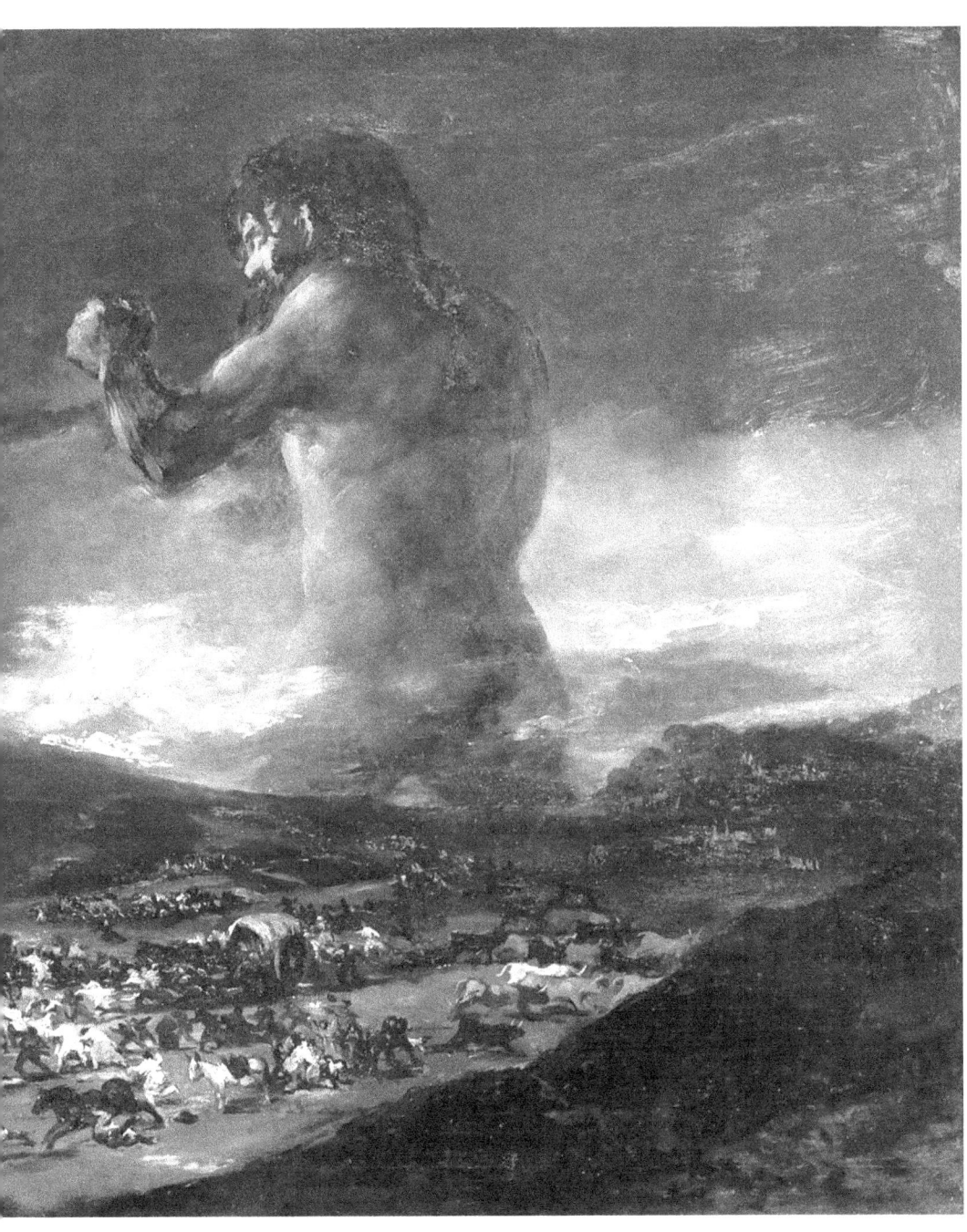

Francisco Goya, The Colossus, 1818-25, Madrid

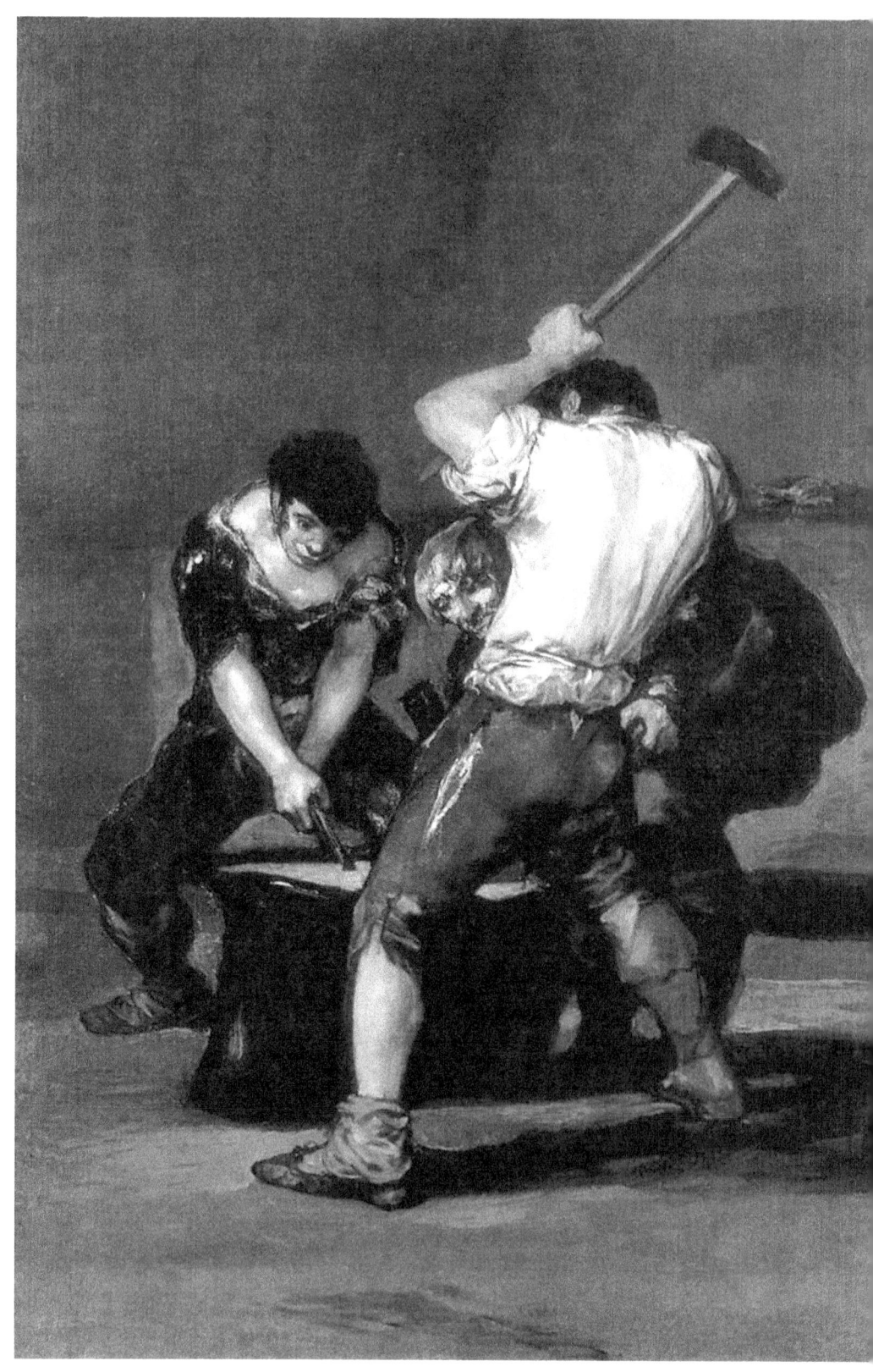

Francisco Goya, The Forge, 1812-16

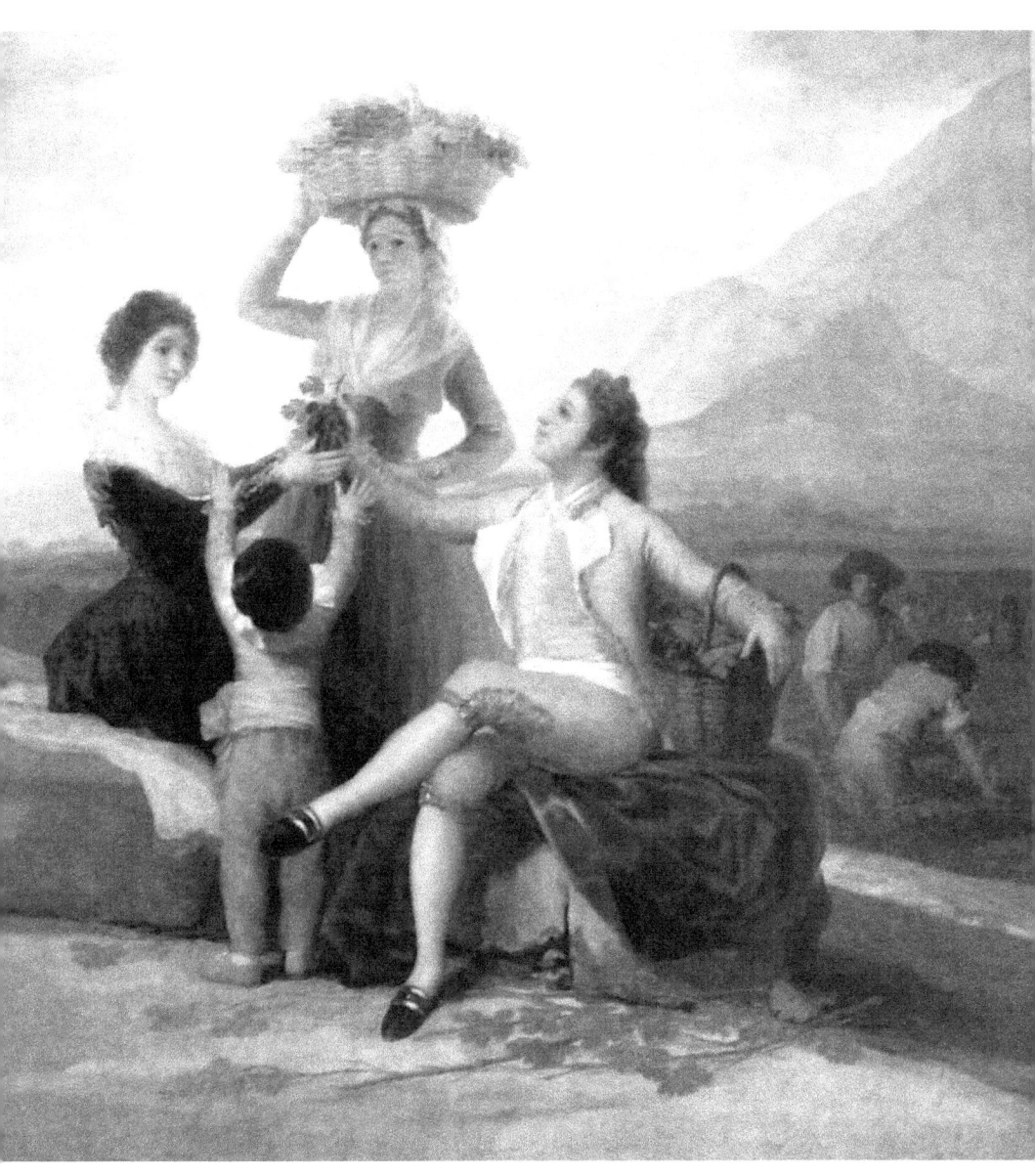

Francisco Goya, The Grape Harvest, 1794, Madrid

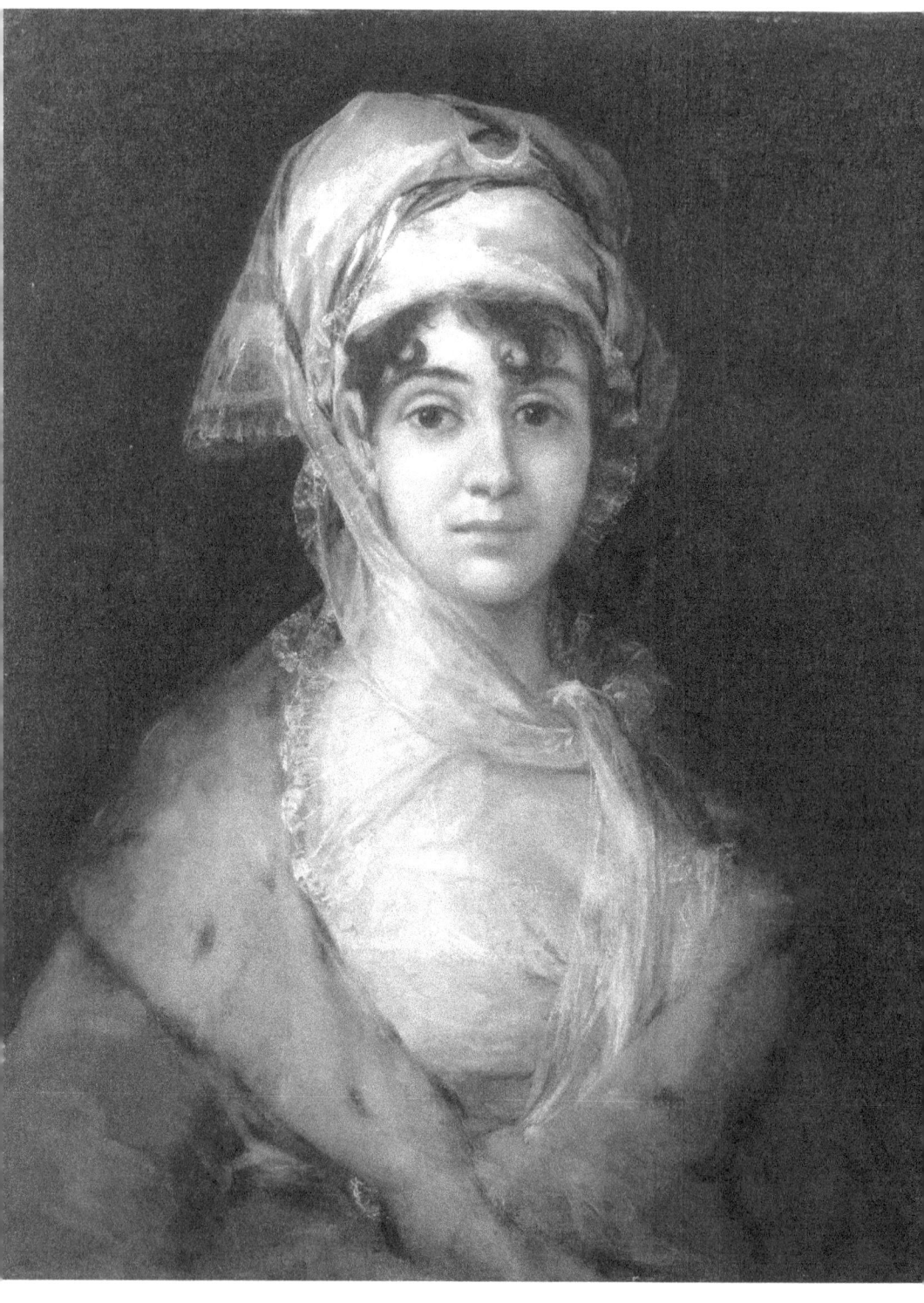

Francisco Goya, Portrait of the Actress Antonia Zarate, 1811, Hermitage Museum

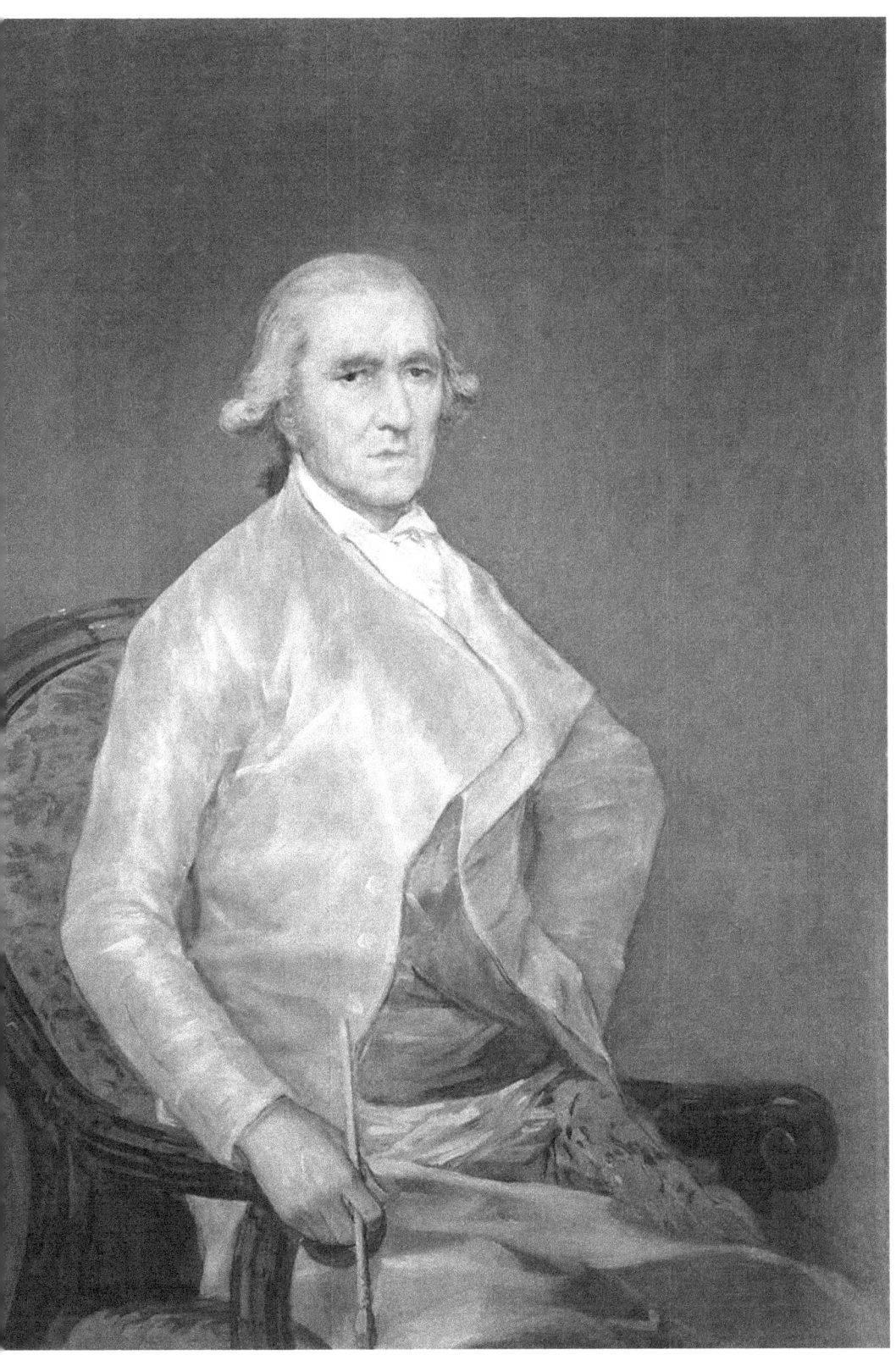

Francisco Goya, Portrait of Francisco Bayeu, 1795, Madrid

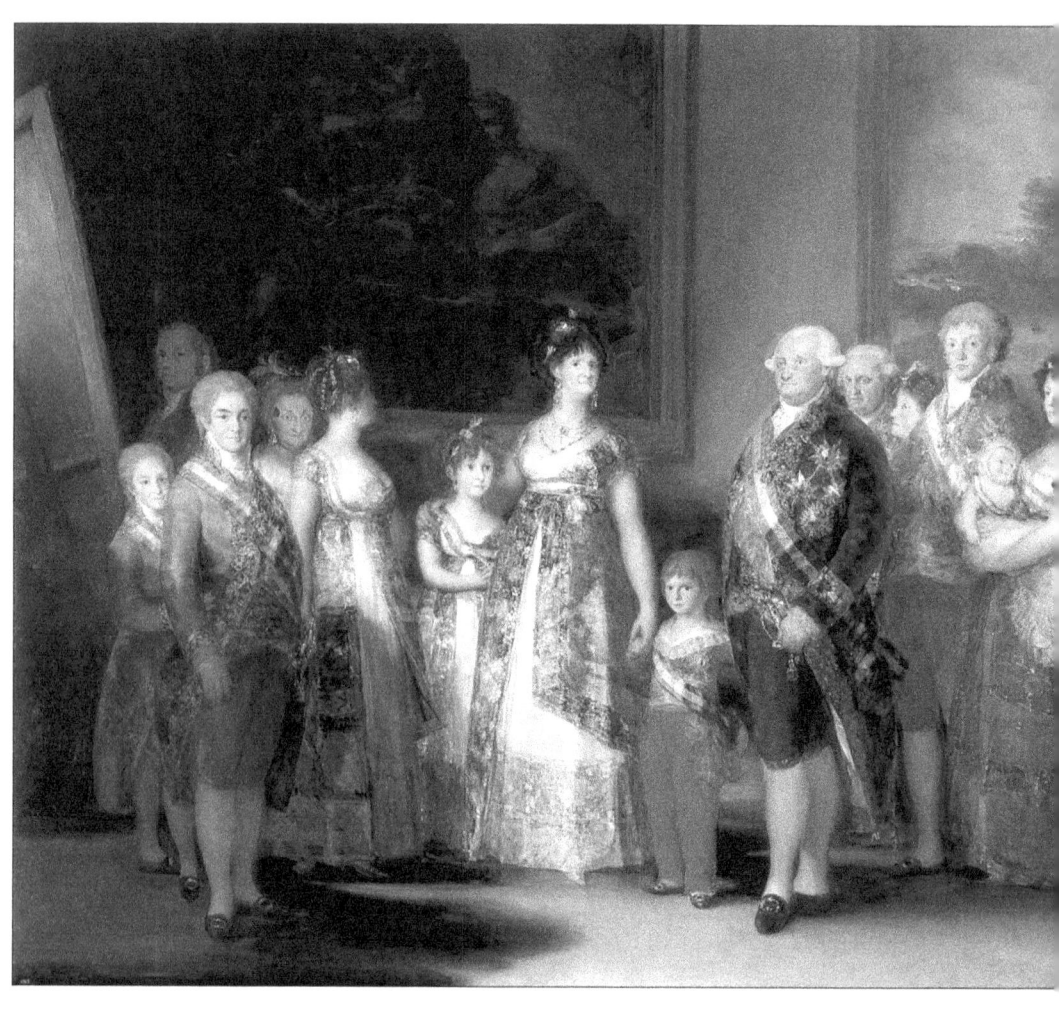

Francisco Goya, The Family of Charles V, Madrid

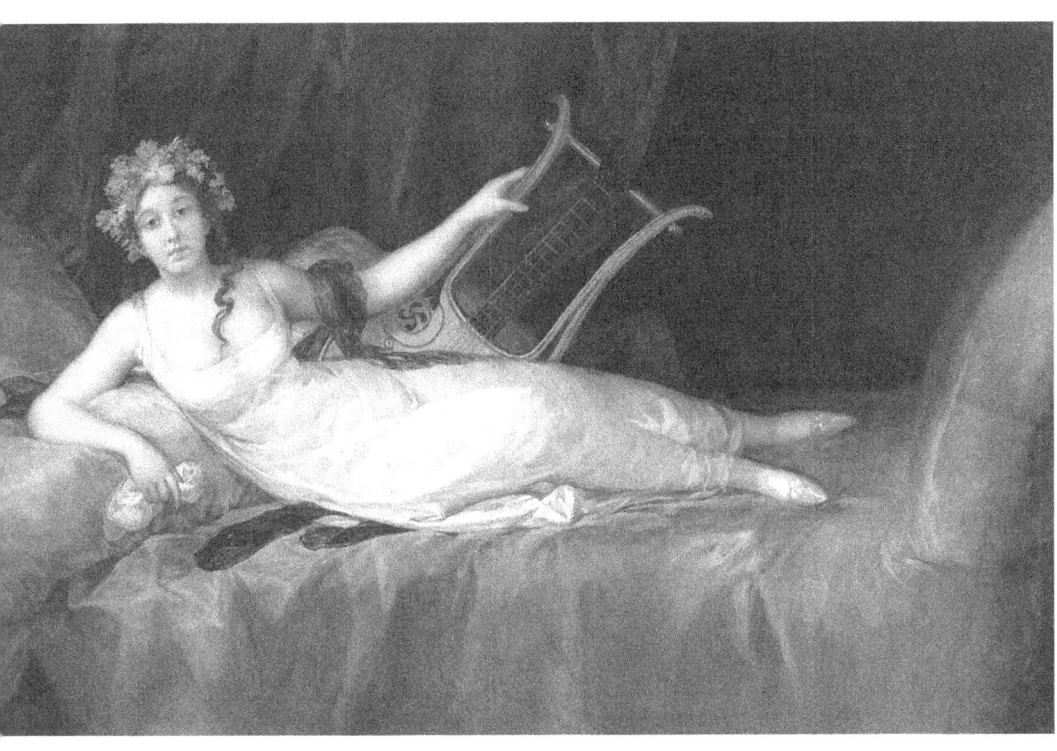

Francisco Goya, Retrato de la Marquesa de Santa Cruz, Madrid

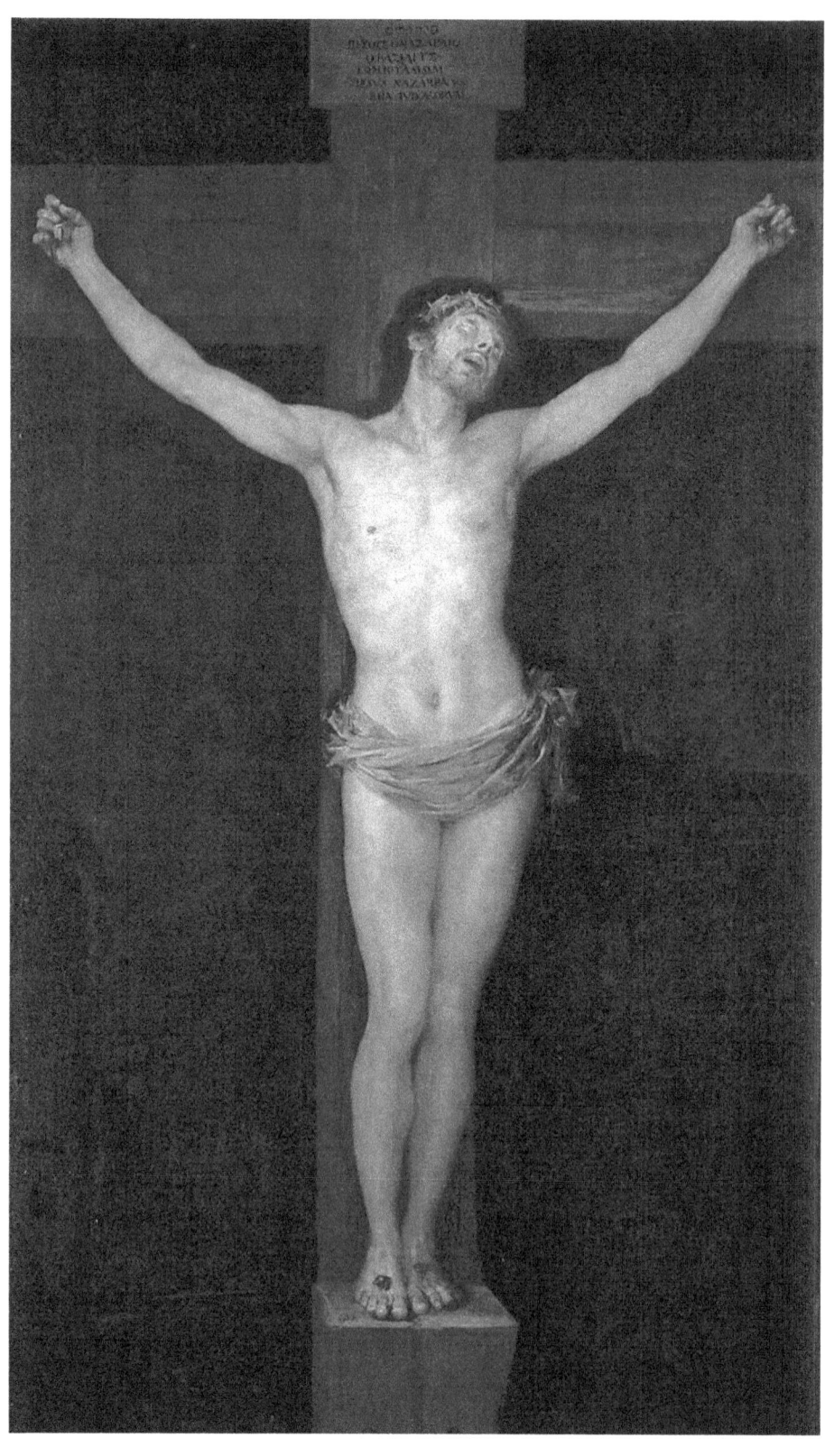

Francisco Goya, Christ On the Cross, 1780, Madrid

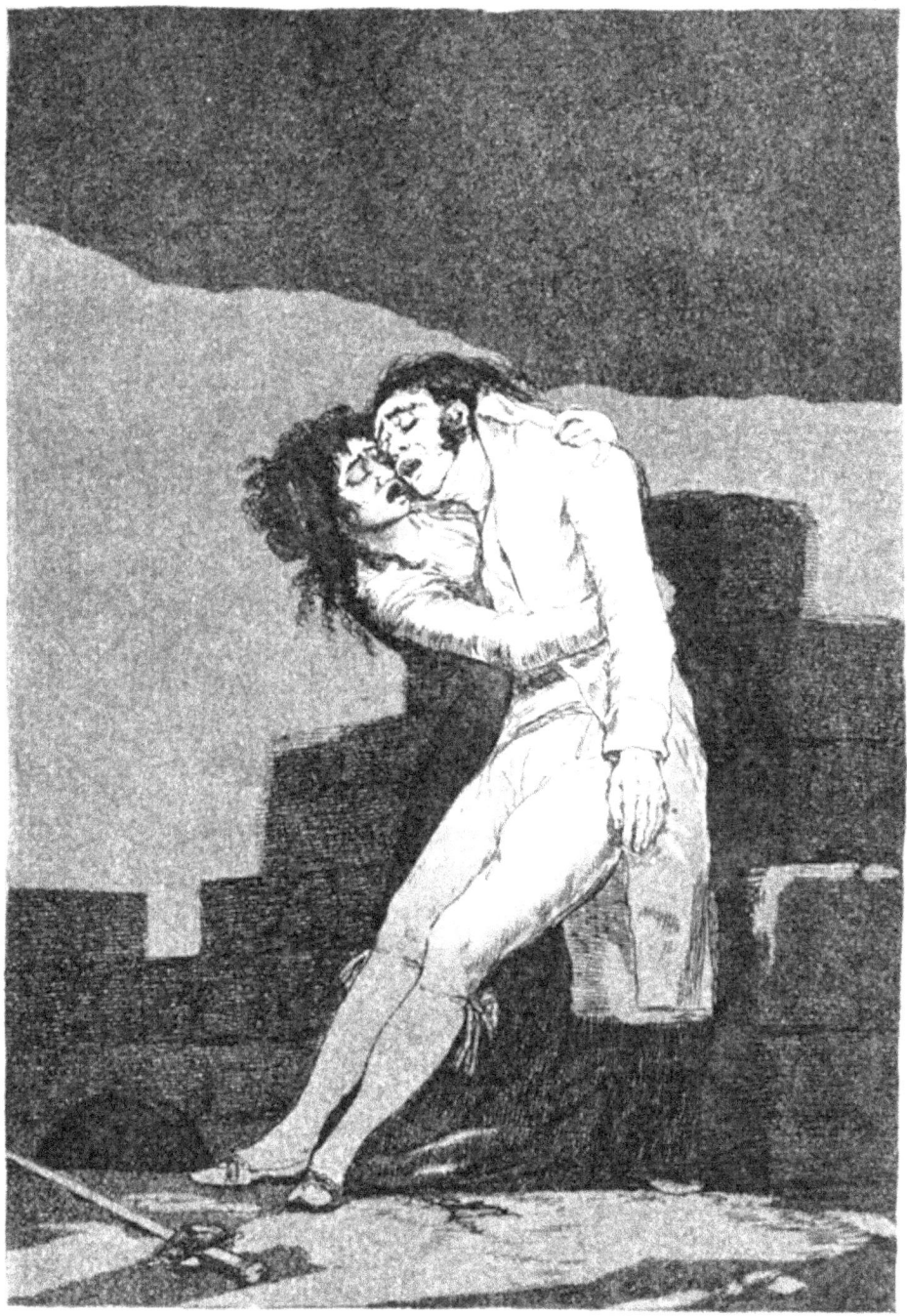

El amor y la muerte

Francisco Goya, Love and Death, 1799

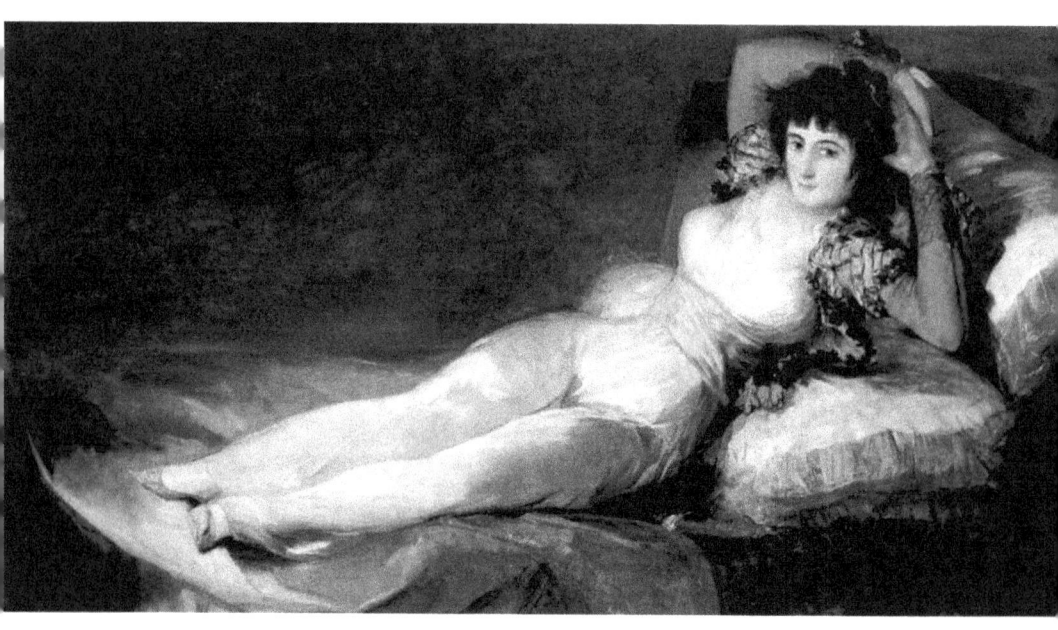

Francisco de Goya, Clothed Maya, 1801

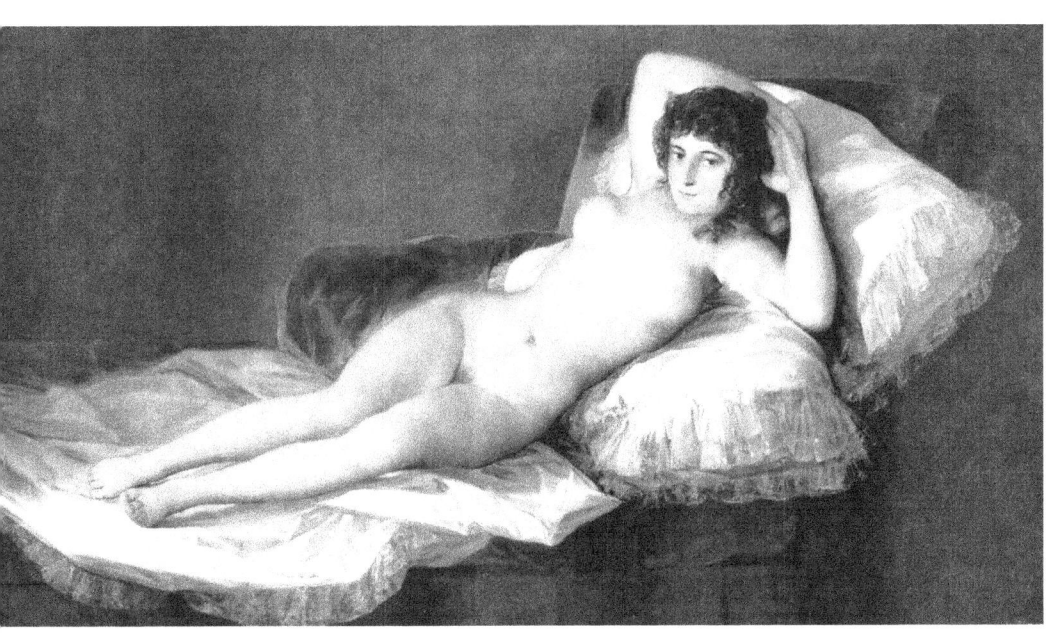

Francisco de Goya, Naked Maja, c. 1801, Prado, Madrid

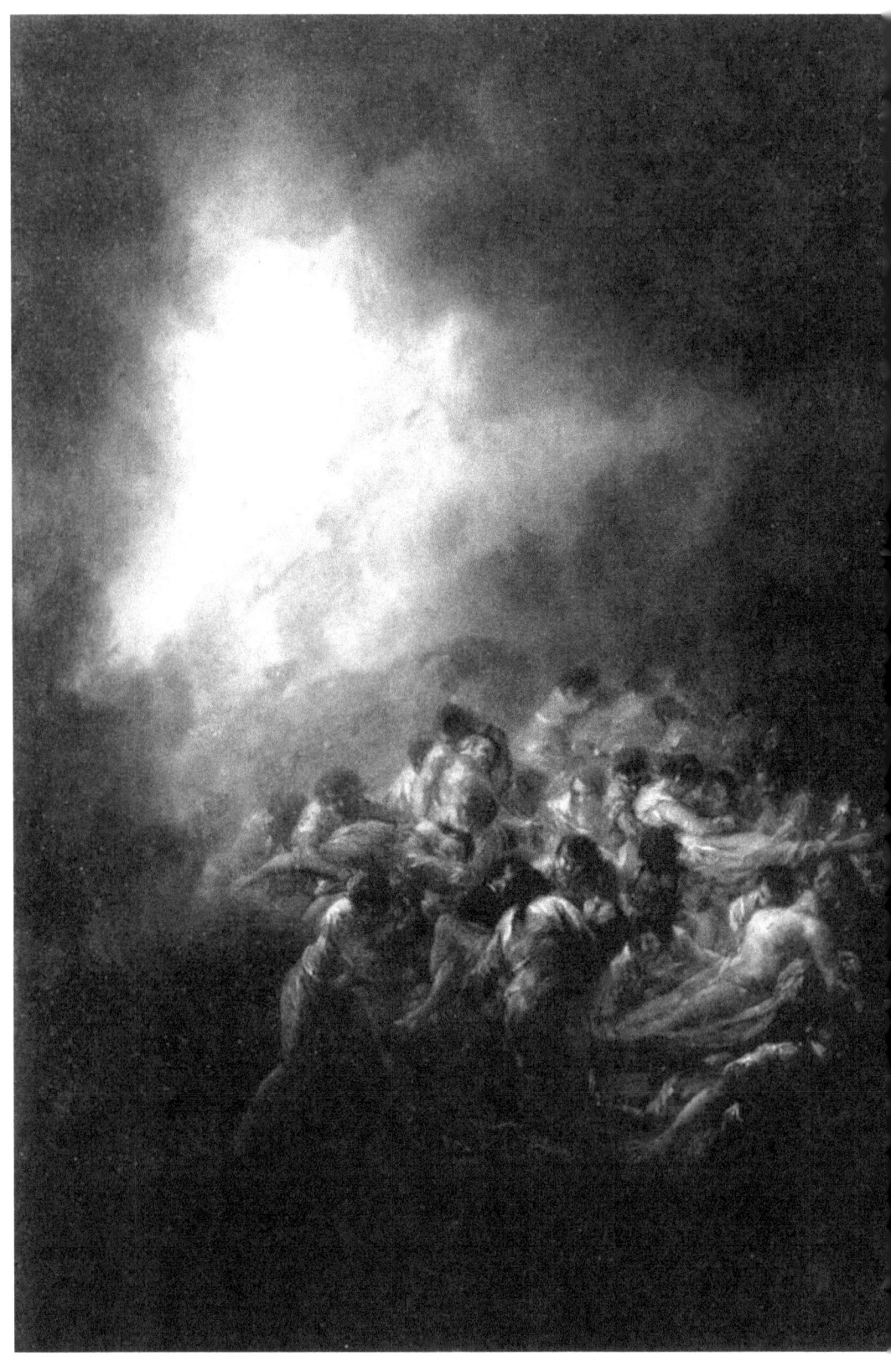

Francisco Goya, A Fire, 1793, private collection

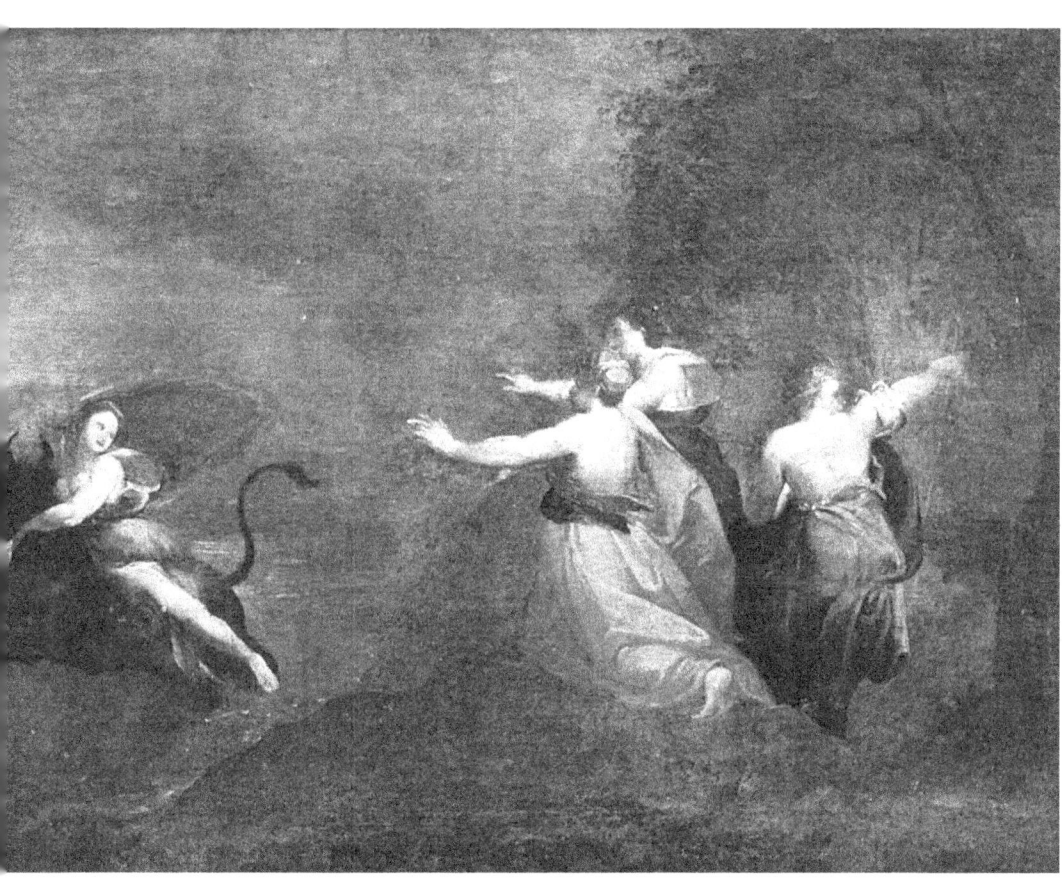

Francisco Goya, The Rape of Europa, 1772

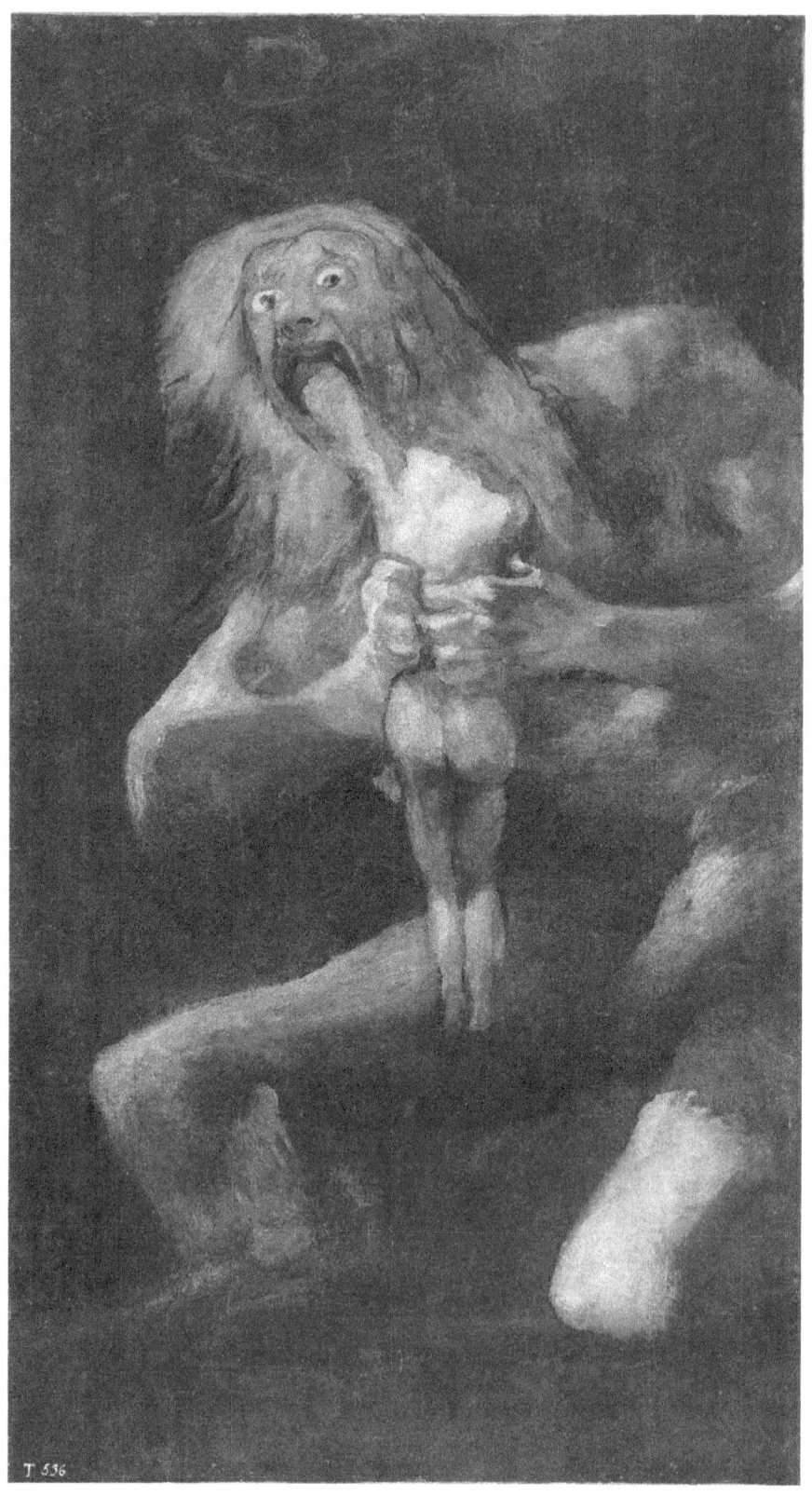

Francisco Goya, Saturno devorando a su hijo, 1819-1823, Madrid

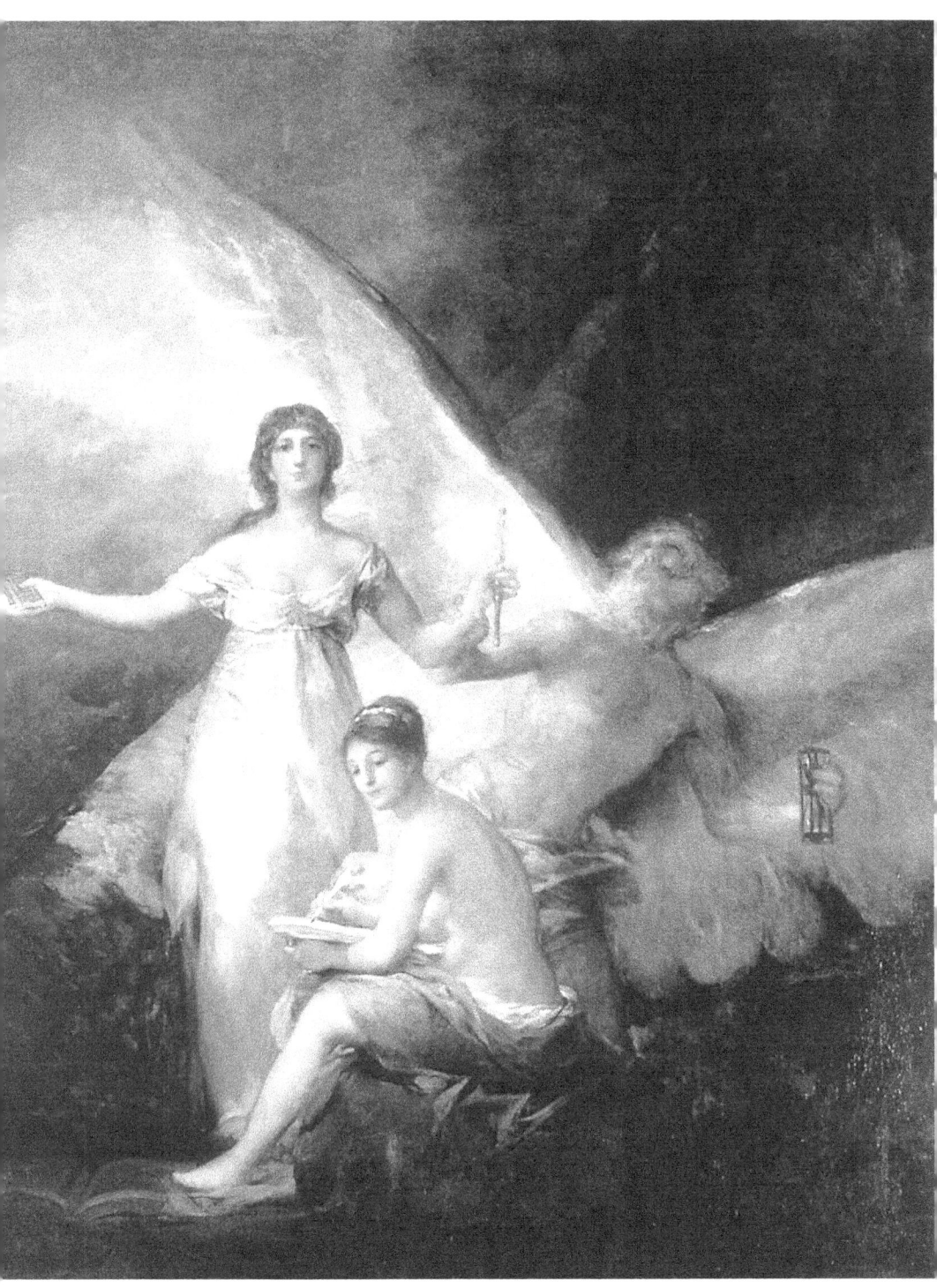

Francisco Goya, La Verdad, el Tiempo y la Historia, 1797-1800

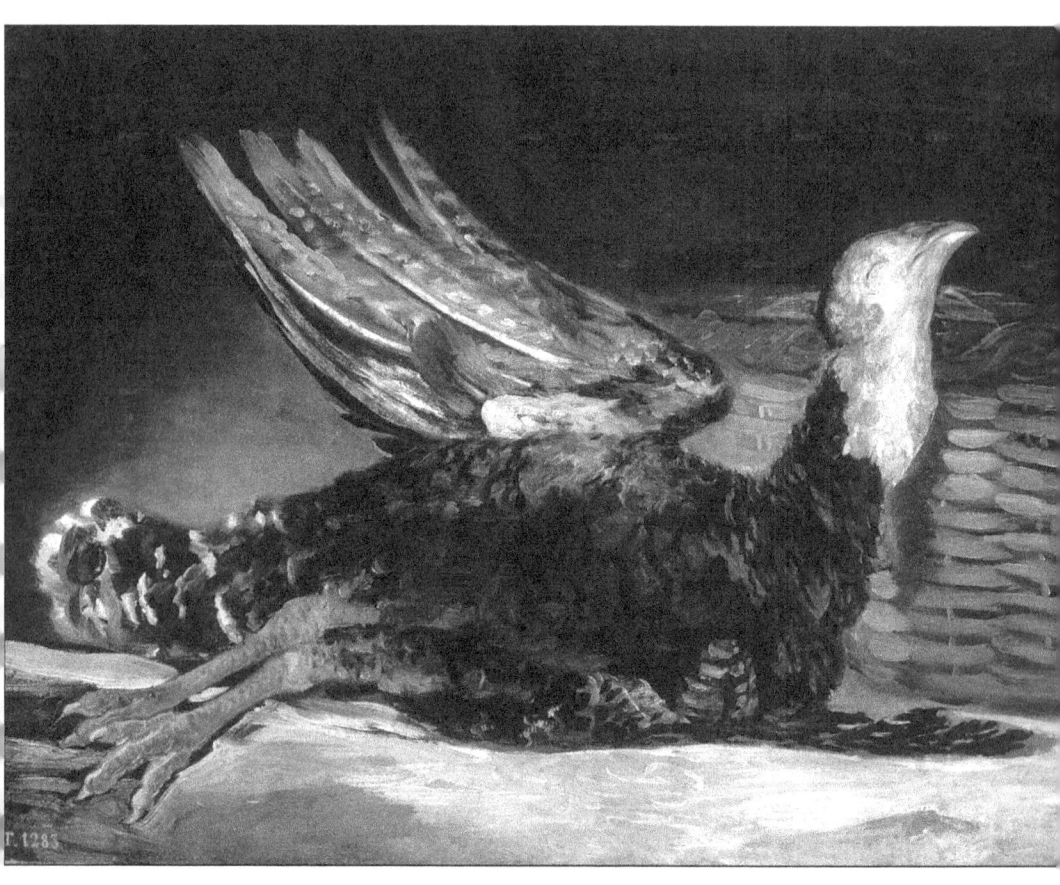

Francisco Goya, Dead Bird, 1808-12, Madrid

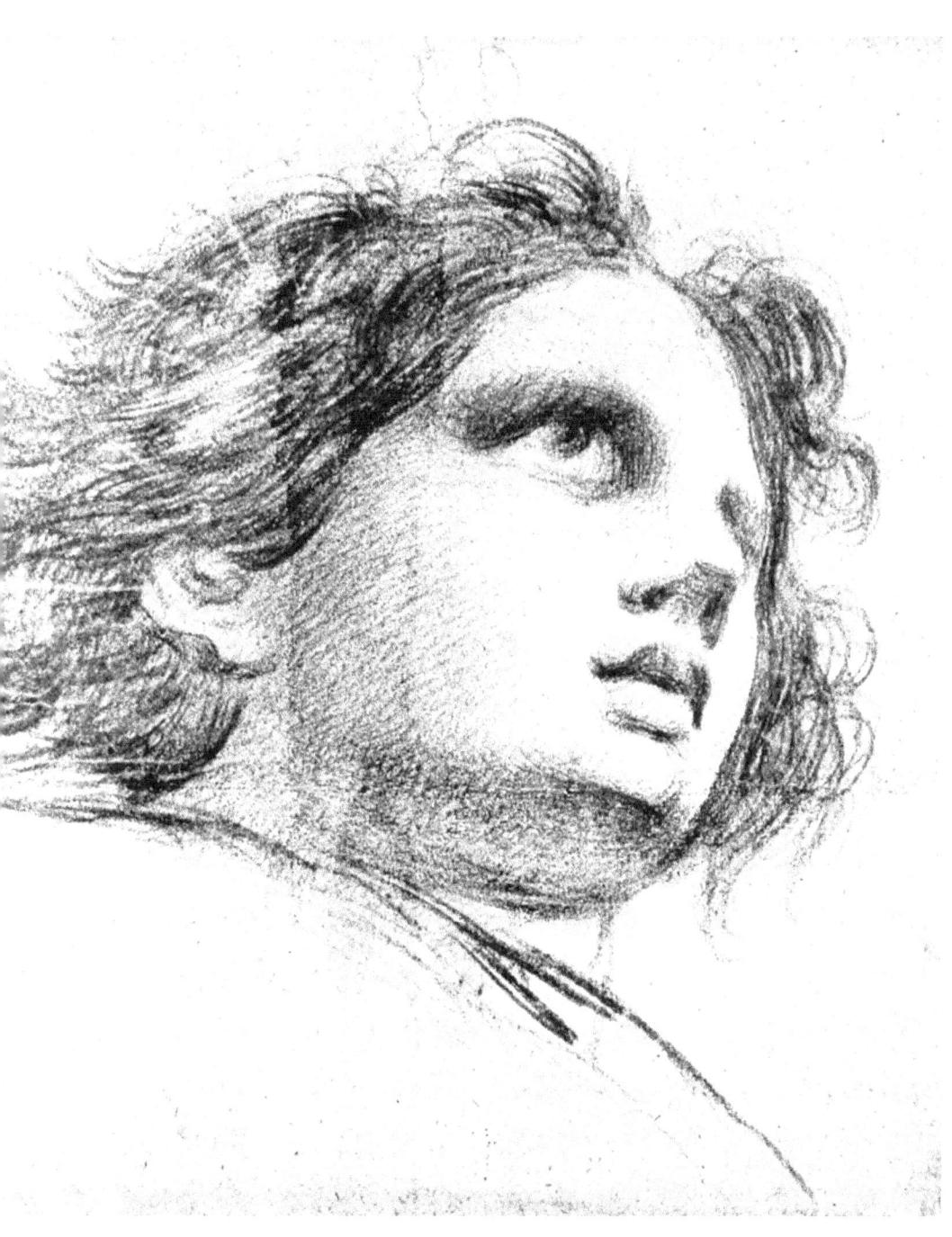

Francisco Goya, Head of an Angel, 1772

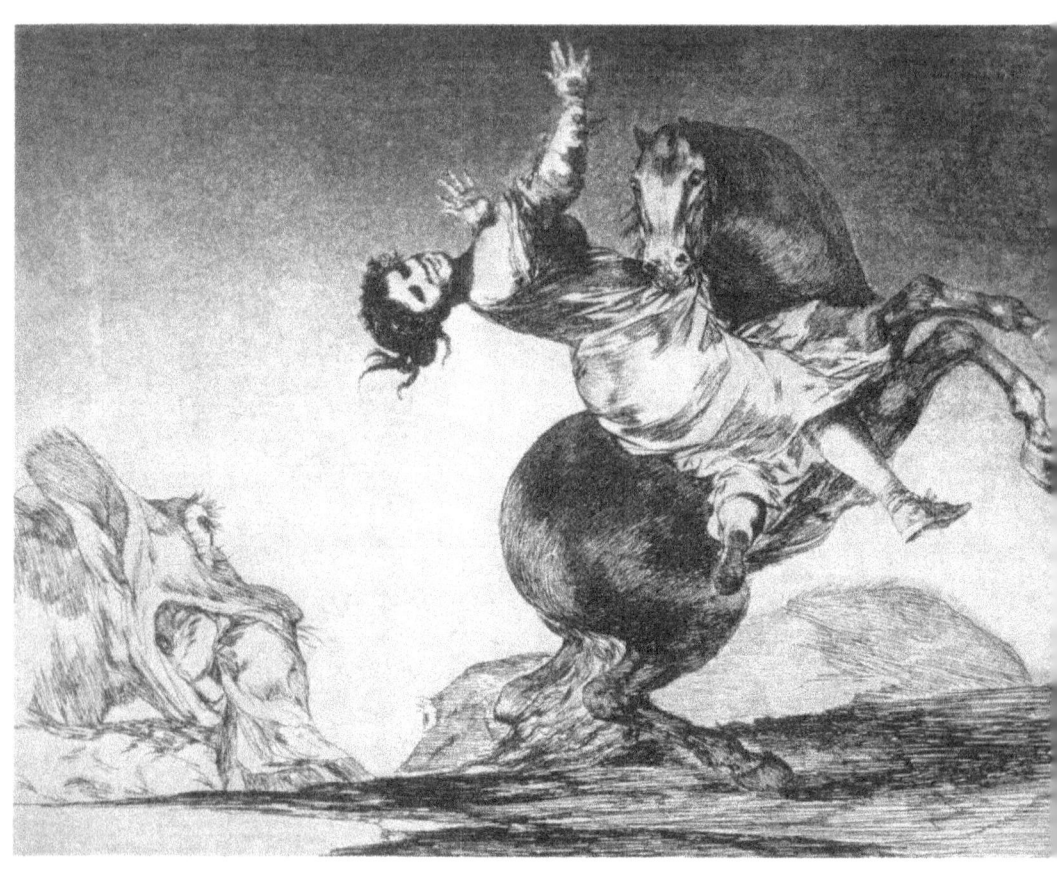

Francisco Goya, Unbridled Follishness, 1819-23

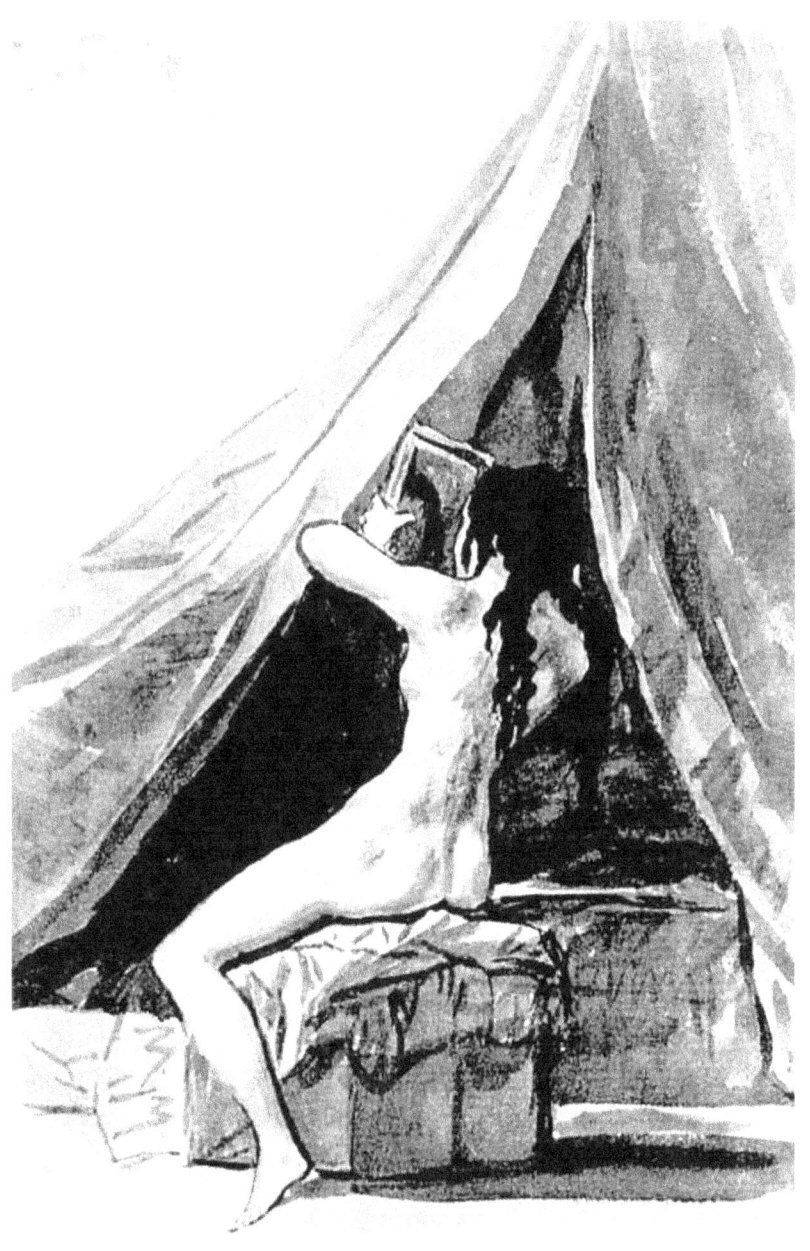

Francisco Goya, Nude, 1796-97

THE GLORIOUS PERIOD

At the same time that he was painting his frescoes and his scenes of popular life, Goya also tried his skill at portraiture. In this branch of his art his success was immediate and complete. From his very first attempts he attained the highest possible reputation. From morning till night he saw his studio besieged by all the most distinguished figures in the society of the Court and the city. It soon became the fashion, the rage, to have oneself painted by Goya. They stood in line at his door; they brought all sorts of influence to bear to obtain the favour of a sitting. All the celebrities of the period, poets, scientists, political luminaries, equally with ladies of rank and reigning beauties, succumbed to this unheard-of vogue, which persisted, we may add, to the very end of the master's long career. Furthermore, his portraits form the most extensive part of his life-work, and at the same time the part which is the most indisputable and the most perfect.

There are nearly two hundred portraits that are known to have been painted by Goya. They are not all of equal value, and in some of them we feel a certain degree of carelessness of execution, which is to be explained by the rapid workmanship demanded of him by the abundance of his orders. But however hasty the work may be, there are always to be found in it the essential qualities of this artist: a surety of expression, a free yet firm outline, and an incredible understanding of his model's personality. Goya did not trouble himself to embellish his patrons, for he was no flatterer; if the man or woman who posed before him was homely, Goya's pencil would do nothing towards correcting the injustices of nature. That was not his business; but he was able, with an unsurpassed clearness of vision, to catch upon his canvas that flashing glance, that fugitive gleam of the inner soul which, at some precise moment, is sure to transfigure the most unlovely features. What distinguished him above all else was his originality, that purely personal stamp, thanks to which it is impossible not to recognize a Goya from the first instant. There is in him something that he shares in common with all the great portraitists, and yet he resembles no one of them. He is Goya.

In the portraits painted in costume, now to be seen in the museum at Madrid, he somewhat approached the manner of Velazquez; under this class might be mentioned the portraits of the Infante Don Luis and his family, that of the Count of Florida-Blanca, of the Duchess of Alba, and of General Urrutia, which is a magnificent masterpiece. All these portraits possess distinction, bold relief, and a lofty carriage which recalls the free and noble manner of the painter of Philip IV.

At other times his brush took on a milder manner, shading off into soft and vaporous tints that set us thinking of Reynolds and of Prudhon, especially in those intimate portraits into which he has put the greatest spontaneity. In this class belong the admirable *Young Man in Gray*, the painter's grandson – this portrait is certainly one of the most beautiful of all Goya's works – and the famous portraits of Moratin, Boyeu, Josefa Bayeu, the architect Villanueva, and the two *Majas*, both the nude and the clothed, which are said to be portraits of the Duchess of Alba, taken in the same pose but under two different aspects. We may also include among the works of his second manner the two portraits of woman which hang in the Louvre; *The Woman with the Fan*, which is reproduced in the present volume, and the *Portrait of a Young Woman*, which, together with the *Ferdinand Guillemardet*, are the only paintings by Goya which France's chief national museum possesses.

All these portraits are admirably conceived, in a simple, natural form, without superfluous details, and they are freely painted, in a rich and solid colouring, and stand out from the canvas, substantial, harmonious, pulsing with life, against those vaporous and imponderable backgrounds of which, since Velazquez, Goya alone has found the secret.

At this epoch Goya was not only a celebrated painter, he was also a man of fashion, mingling with persons of the highest rank. The Infante Don Luis kept him throughout entire seasons at his palace of Arenas de San Pedro, in the province of Avila, and it was there that Goya executed an entire series of magnificent portraits and genre paintings which belong to-day to the Counts of Chinchón. "Then there are the Benaventes, Dukes of Ossuna and of Candia, who for a period of more than ten years ordered work after work from him, at one time religious compositions, destined for the cathedral at Valencia, such as *St. Francis of Barja bidding Farewell to his Family* a n d *St. Francis exhorting an Impenitent Dying Man*, celebrated pictures which have been reproduced by the engraver Peleguer, – at other times portraits of the family, and lastly, a series of twenty-seven genre pictures for their *Alameda* in the environs of Madrid."

Idyllic and anecdotic scenes play by far the larger part in these compositions. There is an *Al Fresco Breakfast*, in the midst of a delightful landscape, a *Dance beside the Water*, a *Hunter showing his Family the Game that he has Killed*, a *Harvesting the Hay*, a *Resting from Labour*, a *Greased Pole*, a *Comical Accident at a Picnic*, a *Winter Landscape*, *The Seasons*, *Workmen constructing a Building*, *Highwaymen attacking a Stage-coach*, *Gypsies playing at See-saw*, *Bulls in the Arroyo*, and lastly some of those inexplicable "caprices," bizarre fantasies in which Goya mingles sorcerers and horned demons with members of the Inquisition.

Goya frequently introduced Inquisitors into his scenes; he had felt their claws early in life and had borne them a grudge ever since.

The most important and most celebrated canvas in this collection is *The Romeria of San Isidro*. This is the great festival in honour of the patron saint of Madrid. "The whole populace has come to make merry on the banks of the Manzanares, and the vast meadow which stretches from the hill-top where the saint's hermitage stands, down to the very water's edge, is covered by an immense throng, motley and variegated, pressing and crowding around the tents of the acrobats, the vendors' booths, the open-air kitchens, and wine-shops. All this picturesque world is divided into a thousand varied groups; here a circle has been formed around a man strumming on a guitar; over yonder a merry set is forming; there is quarrelling, dancing, drinking; there are meetings and partings, and in the midst of all this swarming multitude we watch the coming and going of pages, troopers, porters, members of the body-guard in their red coats, amidst an indescribable pell-mell of carriages with gaily decked steeds, and of *calesinos* with bodies painted in atrocious colours, which are overturned by the restive mules as they break away. In the foreground, dominating the whole scene, pretty women shading themselves under pink silk parasols, and well garbed personages grouped in easy and unaffected attitudes, form a most ingenious and charming framework for the scenes which are being enacted at their feet. In the background of the picture, above and beyond the Manzanares, we see the palace with its terraced gardens and the city with its towers and domes. Here are San Francisco el Grande and the Cuesta de la Vega, and yonder is the famous Barrio de Lavapiés."

Treated in a warm and luminous scale of colour, lustrous with subtle and vivid tones, this sparkling page remains unsurpassed, because of the infinite care which Goya expended in order to give variety and an astonishing degree of precision to even the minutest of its multifold details.

The pictures of country life, such as the *Al Fresco Breakfast*, *The See-saw*, *The Dance*, *The Picnic*, show us Goya under still another aspect. The first time that one sees these pictures in the *Alameda* one would say that they were the product of the brush of some one of the French painters of the eighteenth century; one is tempted to attribute them to Watteau or Fragonard; and it is true that Goya chose, like them, to reproduce the fashions and frivolities of his time; but even while he imitated the vanities and affectations of these masters, he remained nevertheless a Spaniard, and his types and his costumes are represented with the most scrupulous truth.

On the 25th of April, 1789, a few months after Charles IV. ascended the throne, a royal order raised Goya to the dignity of *Pintor da Camara*, which corresponded to *Peintre Ordinaire du Roi*, a title formerly bestowed upon French artists. This distinction gave him, as in the case of Gentlemen of the Bed-chamber, free entry to the palace. Under the new king the Court had taken on a new aspect. During the reign of the devout Charles III. it was constrained to all the outward show of austere piety which recalled the morose years under the monarchs of the House of Austria. Under the new king everything was changed, laughter was revived, festivals recommenced, and with them, intrigues of gallantry and licentiousness. Scandals multiplied, and the example came from high up; Queen Maria-Luisa herself set the pace for a society that had been parched with thirst for pleasure, and she flaunted before the whole nation her absolute contempt of decency and her unbridled appetite for dissipation. The epoch of the high favour of the Prince de la Paix began. Goya, whose marriage had but poorly reformed him, welcomed this change of regime with enthusiasm. He was already something more than celebrated in Madrid because of his prowess with the fair sex, famous for his duels, an adept at all the nicer usages through his constant association with the upper circles; consequently he felt himself fully at ease in this atmosphere of shamelessness and incontinence. He had some famous intrigues and illustrious *liaisons*, which he did not even take the trouble to conceal. Possessed of a caustic and subtle wit, and untroubled by scruples, he was much sought after for the brilliance and the daring of his conversation. Those who did not like him learned to fear him. Before long he had scored an even bigger success as a man than as an artist. Through contact with men of rank, he had acquired not only assurance but a certain air of haughtiness verging upon insolence. Being drawn into the circles of the Duchess of Alba and Duchess of Ossuna, who at that time, like rival queens, were disputing the sceptre of fashion and pleasure, he witnessed and shared in many a boudoir intrigue, taking sides in these women's quarrels, at one time supporting the one side, then again going over to the other, and at last coming out openly in favour of the Duchess of Alba, who at that time was waging a silent warfare with Maria-Luisa. Having become the *cavaliere servente* of the Duchess, he no longer contented himself with plotting intrigues or launching epigrams; but he translated his opinions into the form of satiric caricatures, in which he mercilessly ridiculed the adversaries of his fair lady. The arrows that he launched flew so high that the outraged queen exiled the Duchess from her court and gave the *Pintor da Camara* a leave of absence. Goya and the Duchess set forth side by side on the road to Andalusia, sharing the period of their disfavour on a distant estate belonging to the Duchess of Alba.

This exile, however, was of short duration and only served to increase the artist's reputation for gallantry. The king, who loved him in spite of his follies, recalled him and entrusted him with the frescoes for the chapel of San Antonio de la Florida. The task was a considerable one; it included the painting of a vast cupola and several smaller vaults, tympanums, and arches. Behold then our libertine philosopher transformed once more into a religious painter. Within three months he had completed the entire scheme of the decoration. The subject chosen was as follows: *St. Anthony of Padua resuscitating a Dead Man in Order to Make him Reveal the Name of his Murderer.* Goya placed his saint upon an eminence, from which he calls upon the dead man to come forth; the latter has already arisen from his tomb, has joined his hands, and is about to speak. On the right and left the compact throng press forward, anxious to see the miracle accomplished. All around the cupola the artist has pictured a sort of gallery on which the spectators lean, and among them we see a child with its legs dangling in space. This composition is remarkable in its sense of movement and varied interest. But what distinguishes it especially from other works of its type is that Goya, through an obstinate adherence to realism which cannot fail to cause some little surprise, thought that he was bound to adopt for all the personages in his picture both the costumes and the types of his own time. "His women are true *manolas*, draping themselves in their mantillas, and his men are men of the people, *arrieros* proudly wrapped in their mantles of motley colour. In the corbels of the arches Goya painted cherubim, haloes, and angels, and he endowed these celestial beings with feminine charms and carnal graces that were far too reminiscent of the seductions of the earth. It is related that Goya used the ladies of the Court as models for these feminine countenances, and that on the day when the frescoes were unveiled, Charles IV. expressed his displeasure to the artist in unmeasured terms."

From 1796 to 1797 Goya published that curious series of compositions done in etching and in water-colour which he entitled *Caprices*. And they were quite literally caprices through their infinite diversity of subject and the oftentimes extravagant fantasy of their execution. Scenes of local manners ironically interpreted, mocking allusions to popular superstitions, trenchant criticisms of public men and political institutions, attacks of unheard-of violence upon the established religion and its dogmas, pitiless satires upon the Inquisition and more especially upon the monastic orders, and finally prophetic dreams and visions of the future make up the contents of this singularly complex work which concealed a most audacious motive underneath its apparent fantasy. And all this treated with a sparkling brilliance, a diabolical cleverness that is carried sometimes to the point of brutality, with a realism that often causes a sort of revulsion. As to the execution, it is remarkable: the lines are clear-cut and vigorous, the design is solid, almost schematic in places for the purpose of enhancing the energy; with incomparable art, Goya makes use of contrasts for the purpose of obtaining astonishing relief, perfect modelling, and effects of light that produce the illusion of painting. In these compositions he shows the variety and flexibility of his talent, which undertook with equal felicity the most widely diverse branches of his art.

In Spain these *Caprices* enjoyed a very considerable success, but they caused considerable discomfort to their author. At one time their publication was suspended. The Inquisition, which had been especially maltreated in these designs, became once more threatening, and showed an implacable ardour in its quest for vengeance. Nevertheless, it failed of its purpose, thanks to the kind offices of the Prince de la Paix, who was himself hostile to the monks and took Goya under his protection. In accordance with his advice, Goya offered his *Caprices* to the king, Charles IV., who, acting in accord with his minister, accepted them for his collection of copper-plates. Having thus found shelter behind the august presence, Goya became invulnerable; and the Inquisition had to let its prey escape.

On the 31st of October, 1799, Goya became First Painter to the king. He was at that time fifty-three years of age. Neither years nor indulgences had undermined his robust organism or diminished his talent. On the contrary, it was at this epoch that his manner underwent a transformation which bears witness once again to the resources and the vitality of this exceptional nature. A study of the works of Rembrandt had awakened in him a violent passion for the effects of light and of chiaroscuro, and from this time forward we find him practising this difficult art and manifesting in it a remarkable mastery and originality. In this style of painting, which was new to him, he achieved masterpieces from the first attempt, such for instance as the *Betrayal by Judas*, in the cathedral at Toledo, which might have been signed by Correggio or Rembrandt. The patch of light, which throws into strong relief the suffering face of Christ and the hideous countenance of Judas, is distributed in a masterly fashion and in no wise detracts from the luminous transparency of the shadows.

Mention also should be made, among the works in which Goya ventured upon chiaroscuro, of the celebrated picture in the Escuelas Pias in Madrid, representing *The Communion of St. Joseph Calasanz*, and of the spacious and original canvases with which he decorated the walls of his own home.

We now arrive at that turbulent period, extending from 1800 to 1814, which marked an era of national calamities for Spain. The facts are familiar: as a result of court intrigues, the luckless and unhappy Charles IV. found himself in 1808 forced to abdicate in favour of his son; then came the invasion of Spain by the imperial armies, the odious treachery of Bayonne which made Ferdinand II. a prisoner and a dethroned king, while Napoleon, following his mad dream of universal conquest, placed his own brother, Joseph, on the throne of Charles V.; and finally there came the awakening of invaded Spain and its splendid national defence, resulting in the expulsion of the enemy and the fall of the Empire.

All these years of struggle and patriotic frenzy Goya passed in his *quinta*, where he had shut himself up in complete isolation, taking no part in the events which were shaking Spain to its foundations. This attitude of his gave rise to a great amount of comment. In the eyes of many, Goya was an *afrancesado,* a partisan of the French invasion; but there seem to be no grounds that would justify anyone in offering him such an insult. It may be that, pledged as he was to ideas of justice and liberty, he was not displeased to see the downfall of a corrupt regime, under which Spain had been slowly dying. But that he had looked on light-heartedly at the misfortunes of his native land, and that he had not suffered to the very depths of his Spanish soul, would indicate a depravity which no one has a right to impute to him.

And if proof of this were needed, we could find it in his masterly series of *The Misfortunes of War*, eloquent and melancholy commentaries upon that troubled period, giving a gruesome panorama of military executions, conflagrations, pillage, and famine; in a word, the habitual and tragic accompaniment of a foreign invasion. Could an artist who was indifferent have expressed himself in such pathetic accents? Could a renegade have been stirred to such a point by all these horrors? Furthermore, Goya made no overtures to the invaders. While other Spaniards, willingly or unwillingly, figured at the court of Murat and of Joseph, Goya remained in close retirement in his own house, notwithstanding his natural fondness for adventures and festivities. "But above and beyond his incontestable patriotism, a more generous sentiment, loftier and more profoundly humane, emanates from these sinister pages. What Goya hated beyond all else was war: it spelled iniquity, despotism, and above all, tyranny. Nothing more eloquent than this avenging protest has ever been formulated against the spirit of conquest and the barbarous struggle of nation against nation." In about the year 1814, upon the return of Ferdinand II., Goya added to his *Misfortunes of War* seventeen new plates, the strangest and most daring of them all. This is the last and most strenuous battle that he ever waged on behalf of all he loved against all that he hated. What phials of wrath he poured out against intrigue, conservatism, and falsehood, which stifle liberty and repress human thought! What outbursts against the rogues who strive desperately to destroy liberty and justice! Here is a picture in which hypocrisy has conquered and has confiscated liberty: *Contra el Bien General!* Further on is another, in which truth is in its death agony: *Murió la Verdad!* But she will rise again: *Si Resusitará!* for it is impossible that she should disappear forever. Lastly, as a conclusion to this work, Goya prophesied in an eloquent page the return of a glorious era which should inaugurate the reign of liberty, love, happiness, and peace. And it bore this legend: *This is the Truth!*

But the reign of Ferdinand VII. did not fulfil the generous hopes of the great artist. With this king, the worst days of absolute monarchy were revived in Spain; the triumphant reaction manifested itself by persecutions, cruelties, and tyrannies of the most odious kind. Whoever was even suspected of liberalism was marked for exile or for prison. More than anyone else, Goya's personal prominence exposed him to the attacks of the reactionists, but his very fame protected him. Ferdinand VII., when he received him one day, informed the aged artist that he "deserved exile, and more than exile; he deserved death!" but he consented to forget the past and he reappointed the artist to the office of First Painter. It would seem as though such protection should have sufficed to protect Goya from the machinations and hostilities of his adversaries. But it did nothing of the sort. The reactionary party would not consent that a liberal should escape its vengeance, even though protected by royal immunity; so it continued to hound him by means of secret intrigues and calumnies.

Goya, impatient and irascible by nature, could ill bear the malevolent insinuations, allusions, and contemptuous terms; he found himself stifling in such a poisoned atmosphere. Residence in Madrid had become impossible for him; the greater number of his friends, less fortunate than he, had already been forced into exile; and since the persecution showed no signs of abating, he saw his circle of friends dwindling day by day. At last he made up his mind to leave a native land that had grown so inhospitable and hostile. He asked the king for a leave of absence, and upon obtaining it crossed over into France.

THE CLOSING YEARS

Goya went first of all to Paris, but he made a stay there of short duration. Almost all his friends from Madrid, whom Ferdinand VII. had driven from Spain, had taken refuge in Bordeaux, where they formed a veritable colony. He proceeded to join it and decided to settle down among them.

He did not, however, remain inactive. This prodigious worker, who was now nearly eighty years old, could not resign himself to rest; he once again took up his brush with a hand which his great age could not yet cause to tremble. Besides, he was not well off, possessing scarcely anything besides his house in Spain and his pension as First Painter.

Accordingly, he continued to paint genre pictures and numerous portraits. Those of Don Juan Maguire, M. Pio de Molina, and M. J. Galos date from this epoch. He also painted another of his friends, also exiled, whom he met again at Bordeaux – Moratin, the celebrated Spanish poet, who, carried away by his passion for democracy, had sung the French invasion in eloquent stanzas and now expiated his error in exile.

Besides the portraits, Goya painted some very beautiful miniatures on ivory, and he renewed his experiments in lithography, which he had already undertaken in Madrid some years previous. His four large examples representing *Bull Fights* are masterpieces of colour and of movement.

In 1827 Goya had to journey back to Madrid, in order to make a personal appeal to the king for an extension of his leave of absence. Since he could not persuade Goya to remain, the king freely granted the favour requested; but he imposed one condition, and a very flattering one to the artist: namely, that he would first allow his portrait to be painted by Don Vicente Lopez, at that time *Pintor da Camara*. This portrait is now to be seen at the museum in Madrid.

That same year he returned to Bordeaux and once more resumed his cherished habits and his brush and palette. Many of the works of this later period remained in France, and the museum at Bordeaux possesses a considerable number of them.

Goya still continued to work, but his hands had begun to tremble and he could no longer see without the aid of a lens. His strength was failing and he felt that the end was drawing near. He sent for his son, Xavier, who had continued to reside at Madrid; and a few days later, on the 15th of April, 1828, he passed away in the arms of his friends, at the age of eighty-two years and fifteen days.

Goya was truly a great artist in the noblest sense of the term. He possessed qualities which were at one and the same time substantial and brilliant; he was versatile and original, a spirited genre painter and a remarkable portraitist. "In the tomb of Goya," writes Théophile Gautier, "the ancient art of Spain lies buried; gone forever is the world of the *toreros*, the *majos*, the *manolas*, the contrabandists, the *alguazils*, and the sorceresses, the entire local colour of the Peninsula. He arrived in time to gather all this together and to preserve it on his canvas. He fancied that he painted only 'caprices;' yet what he really did was to paint the portrait of bygone Spain, all the time convinced that he was giving his service to the new ideas and new beliefs."

On the following pages are some contemporaries of Goya.

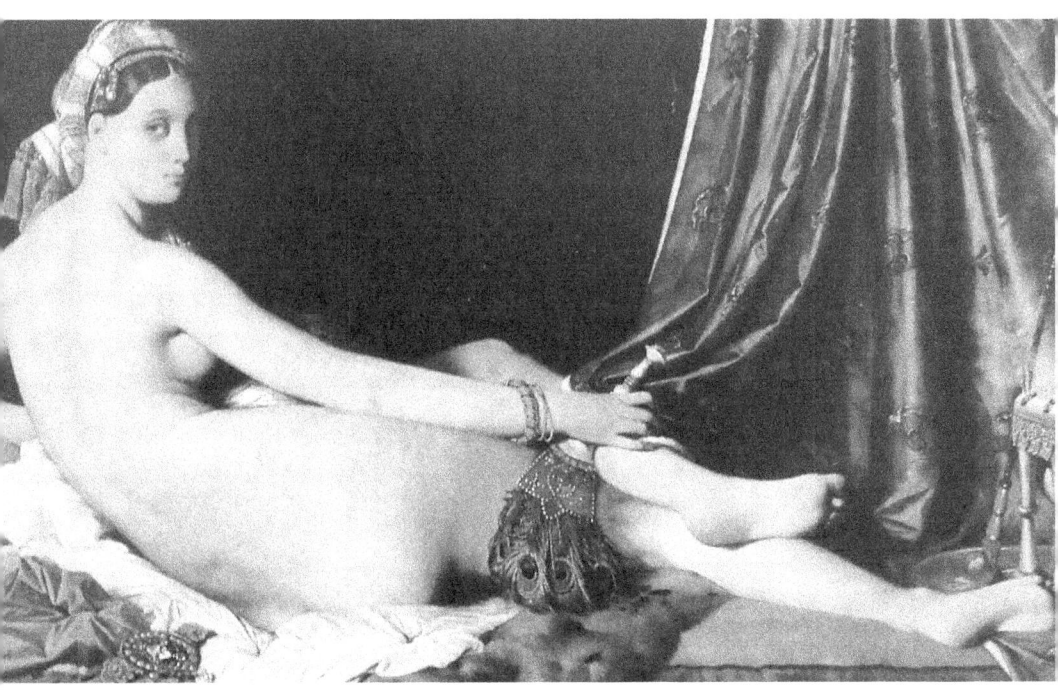

Jean-Dominique Ingres, Grand Odalisque, 1814

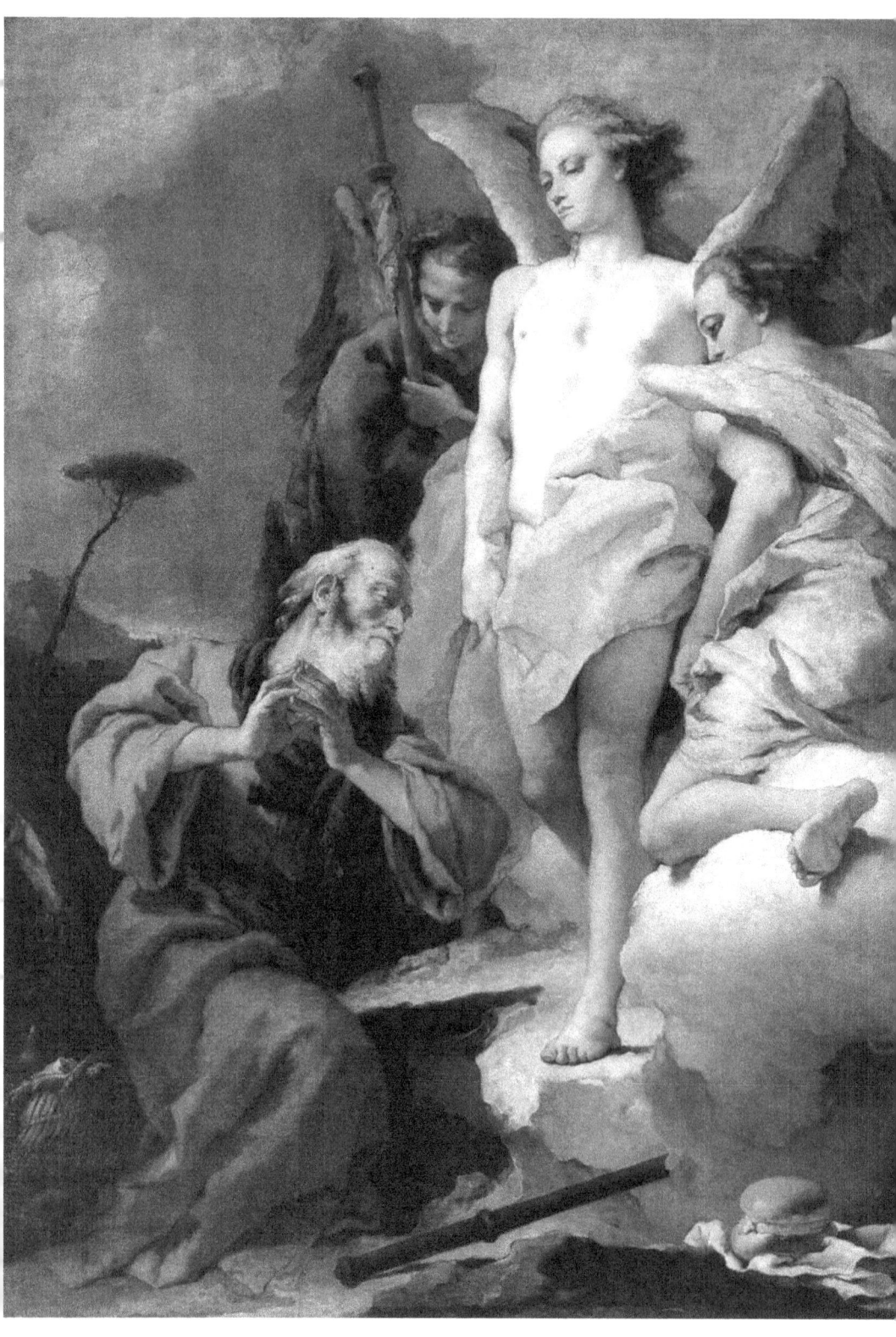

Giovanni Battista Tiepolo, Abraham and Three Angels, c. 1770

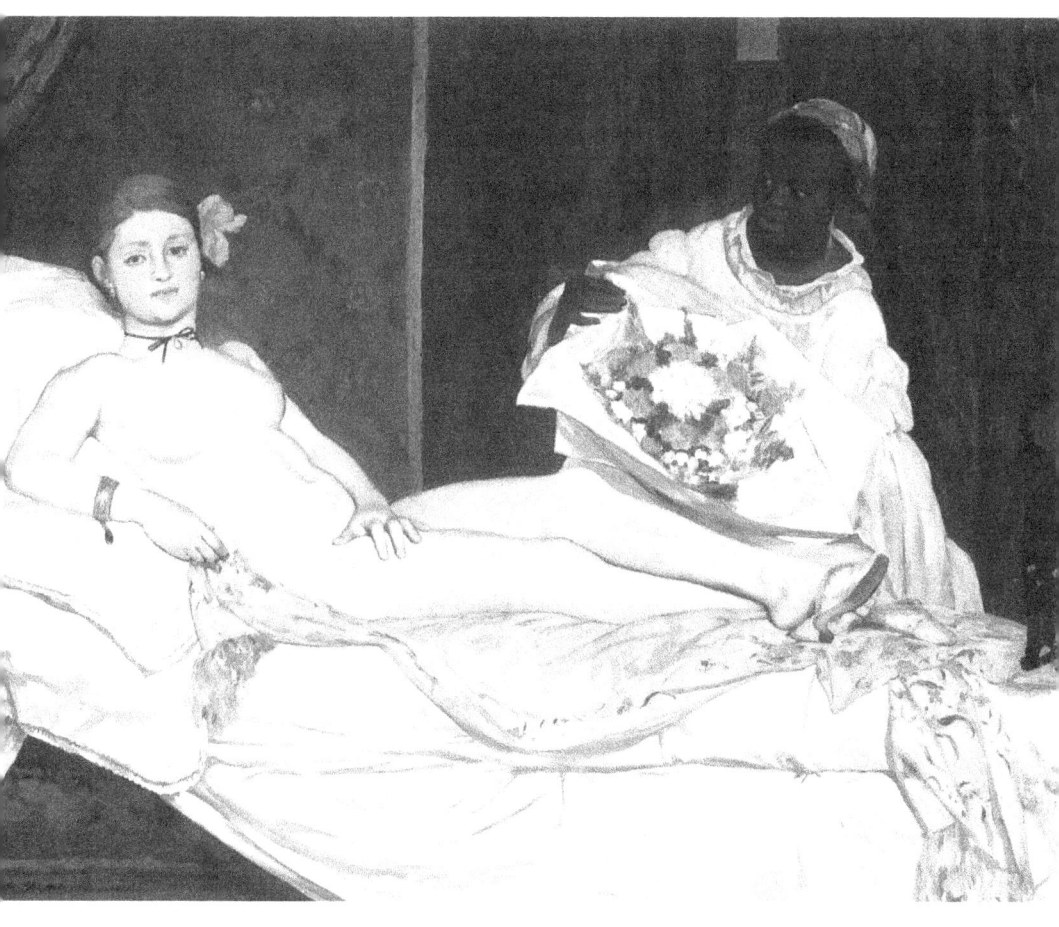

Edouard Manet, Olympia, Musée d'Orsay, Paris

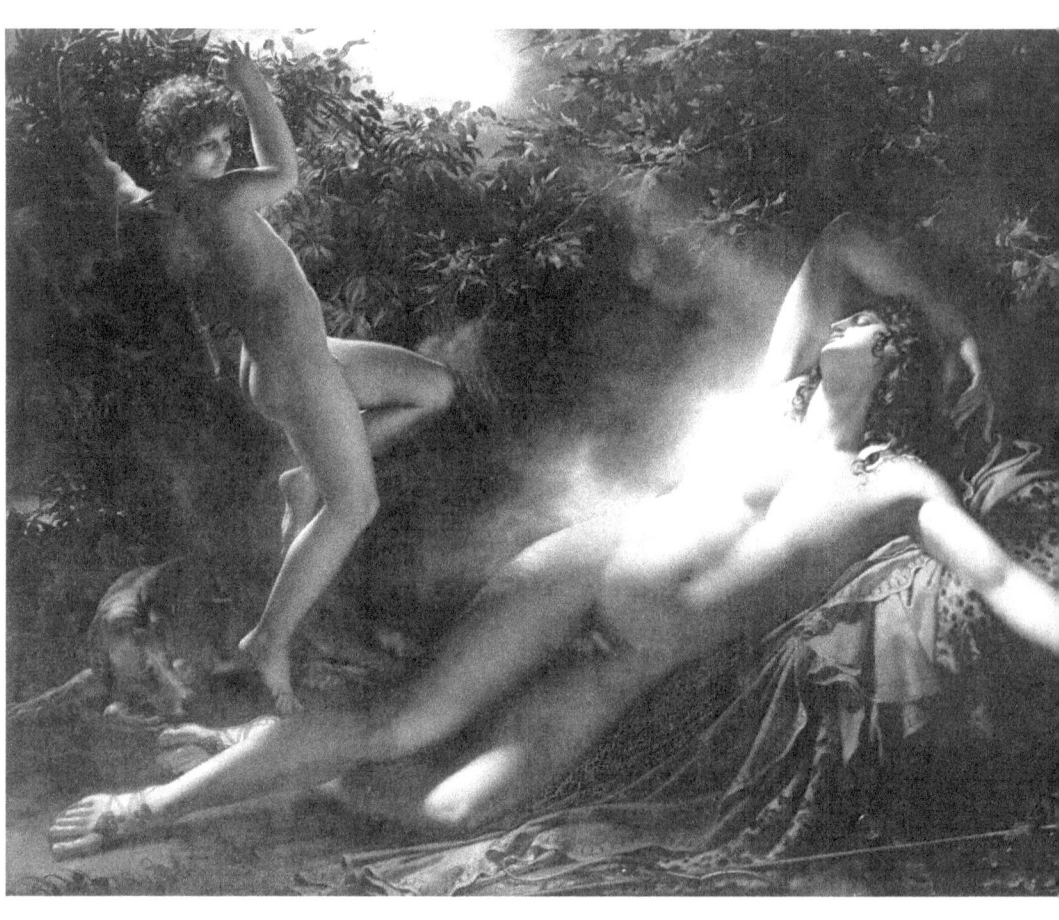

Anne-Louis Girodet-Trioson, Endymion, 1793

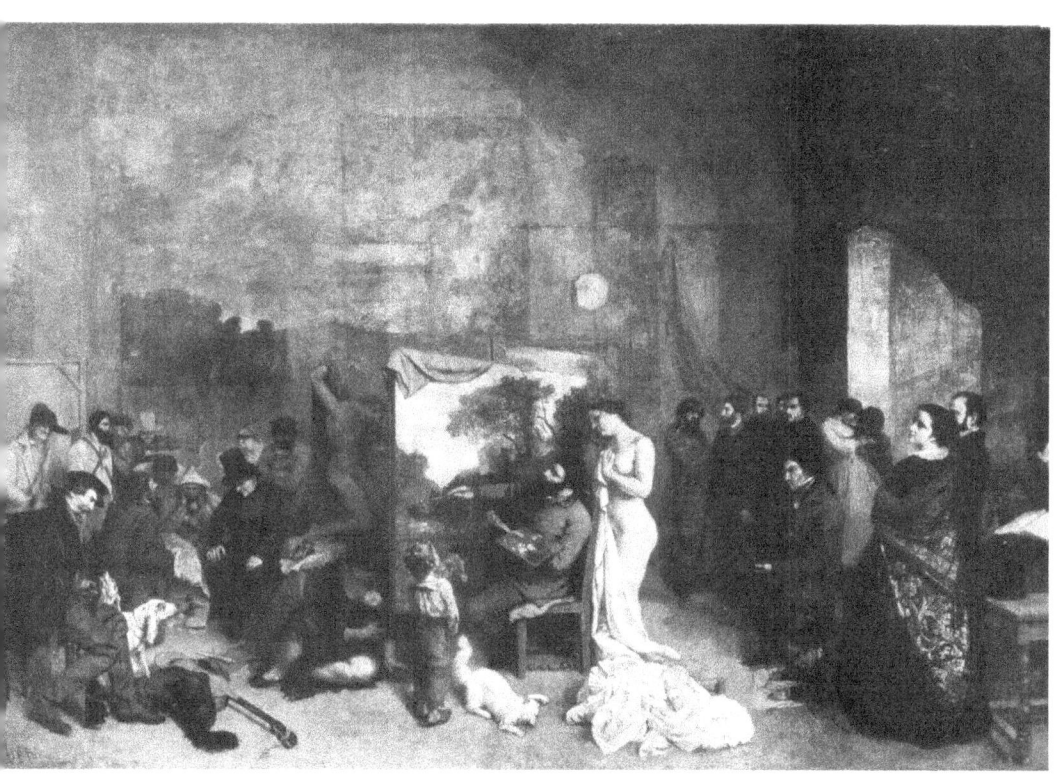

Gustave Courbet, The Studio, 1855, Musée d'Orsay, Paris

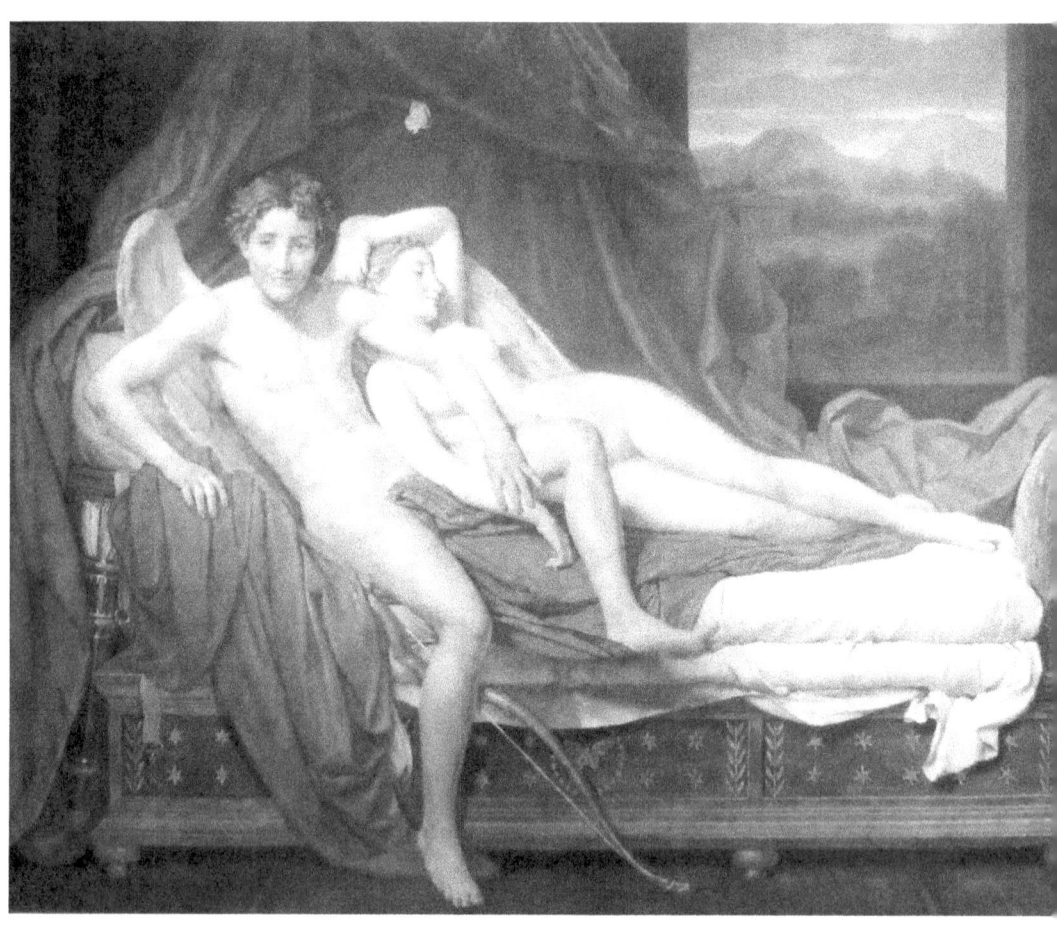

Jacques-Louis David, Cupid and Psyche, 1817,
Cleveland Museum of Art

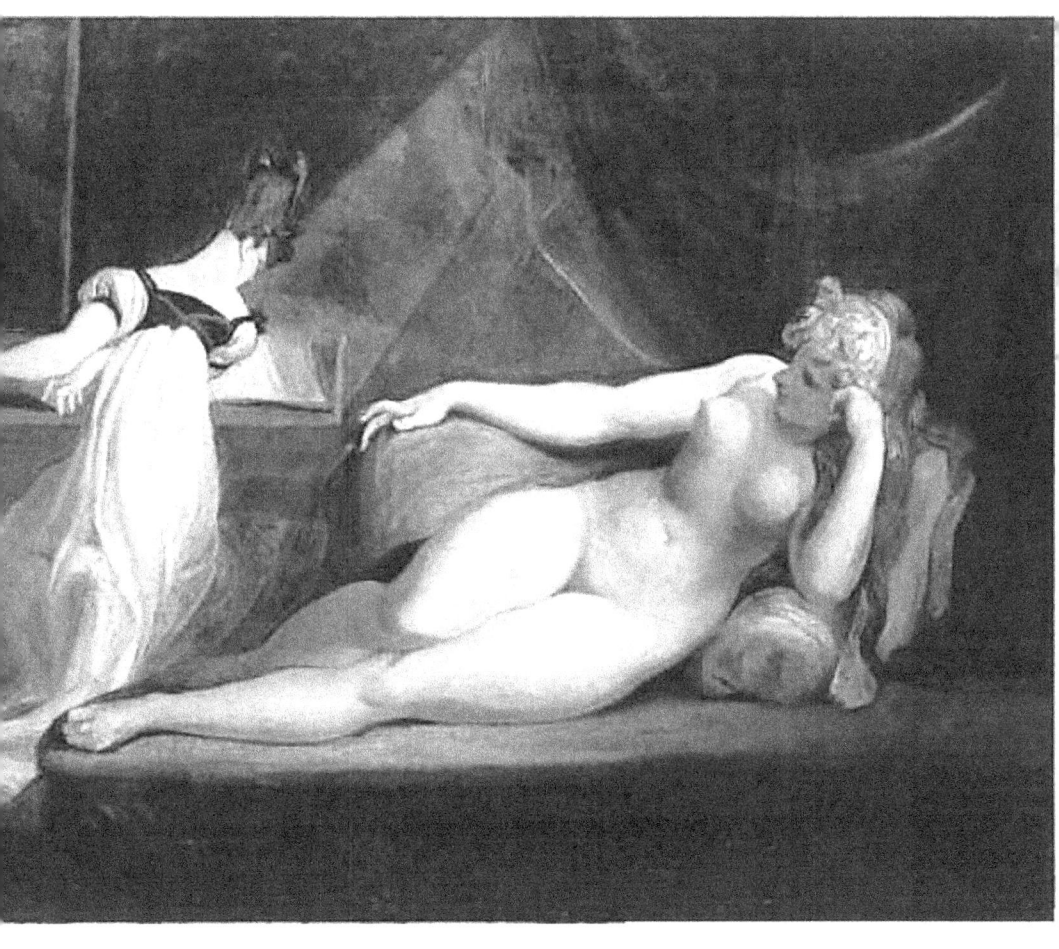

Henry Fuseli

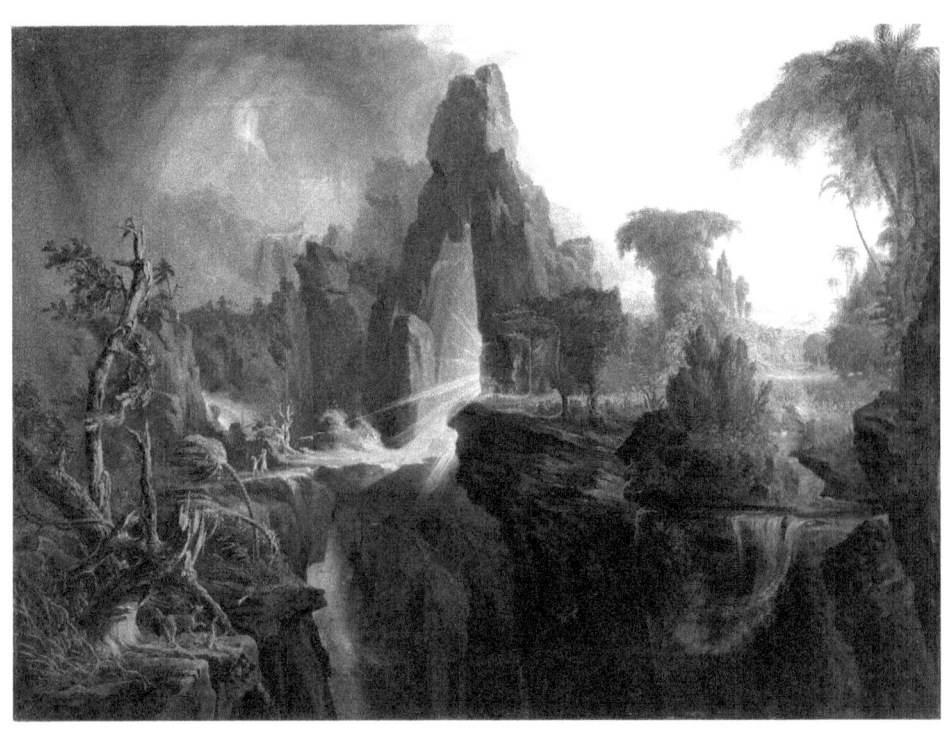

Thomas Cole, Expulsion From the Garden of Eden, 1828,
Museum of Fine Arts, Boston

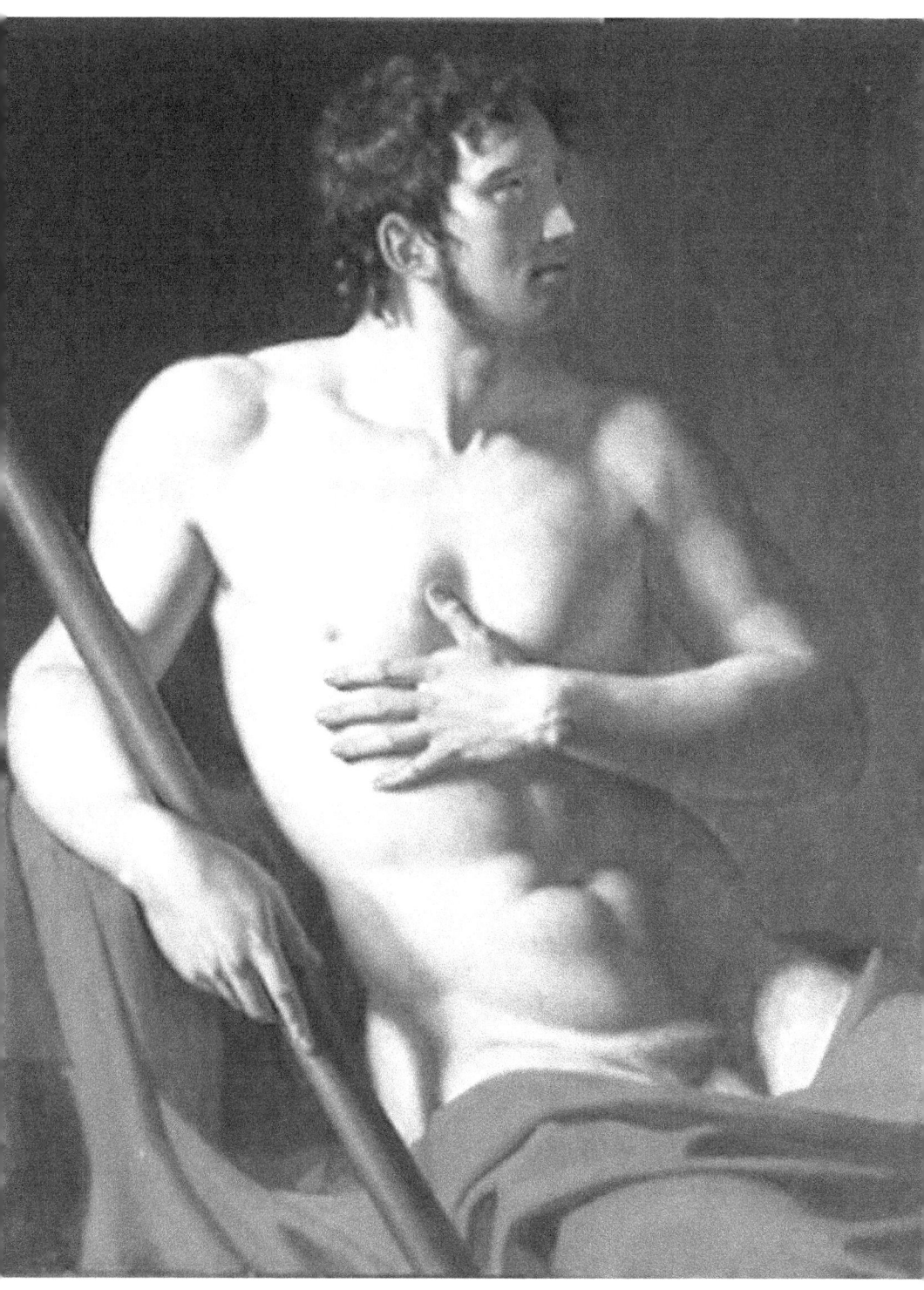

Auguste-Alphonse Gaudar de la Verdine, Male Nude, 1799

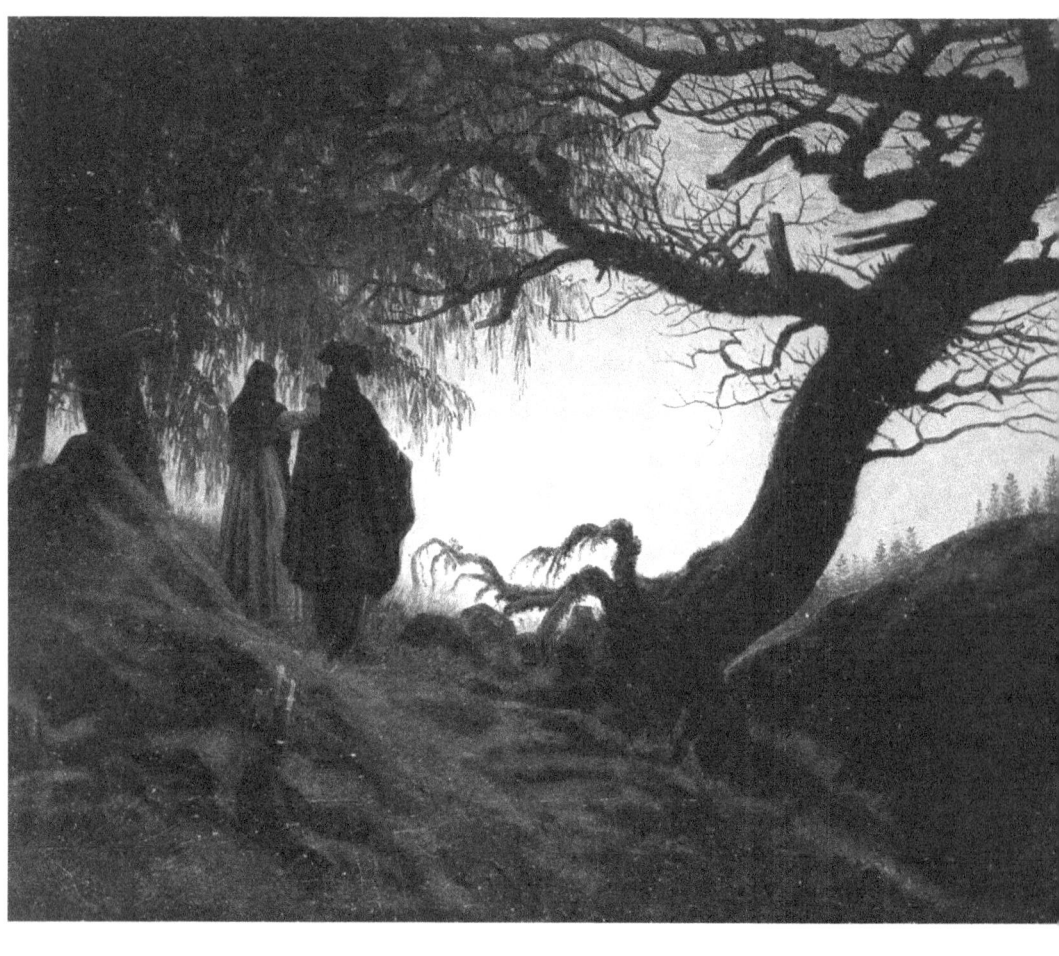

Caspar David Friedrich, Man and
Woman Contemplating the Moon,
1830-35, Alte Nationalgalerie

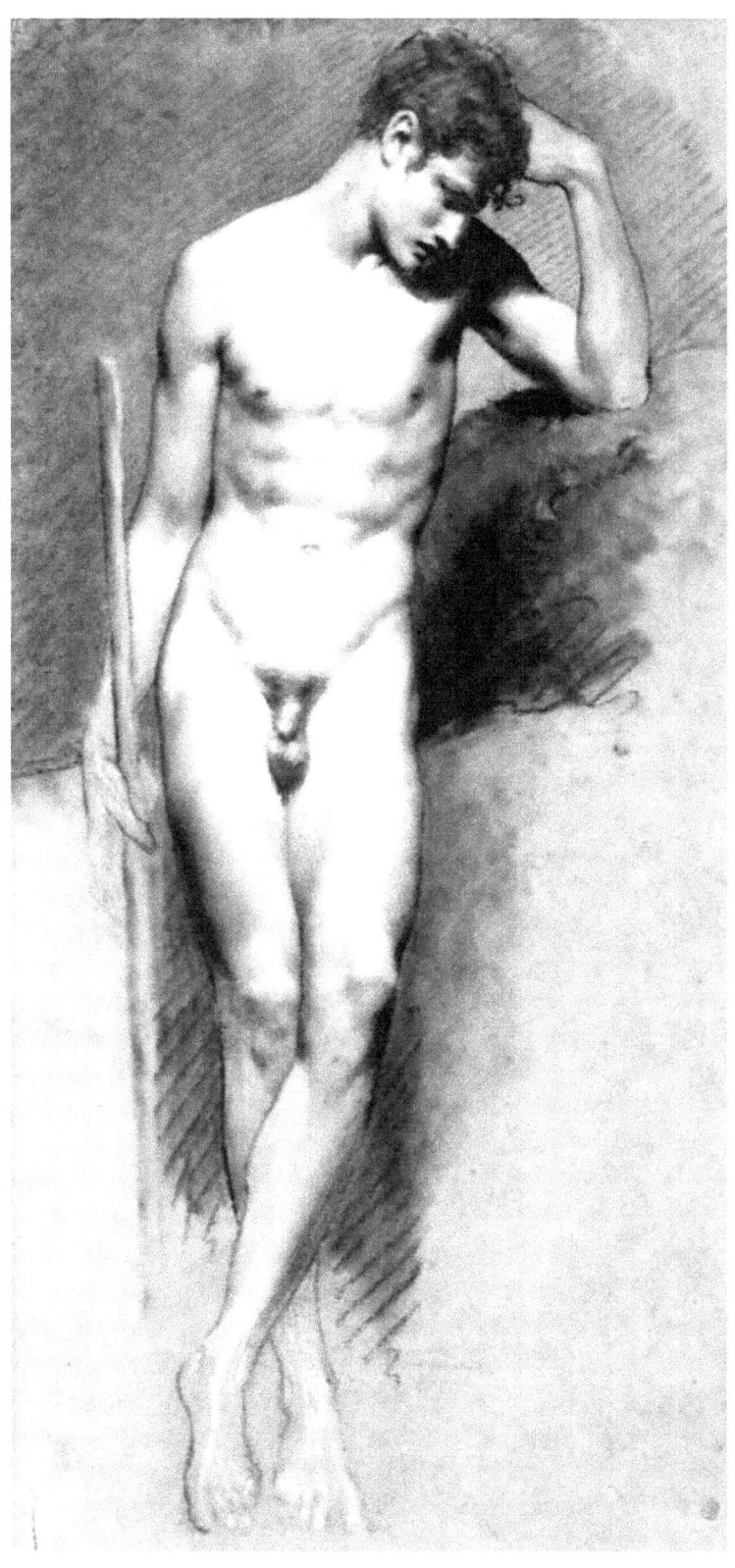

Pierre-Paul Prud'hon (1758-1823), Male Nude Standing

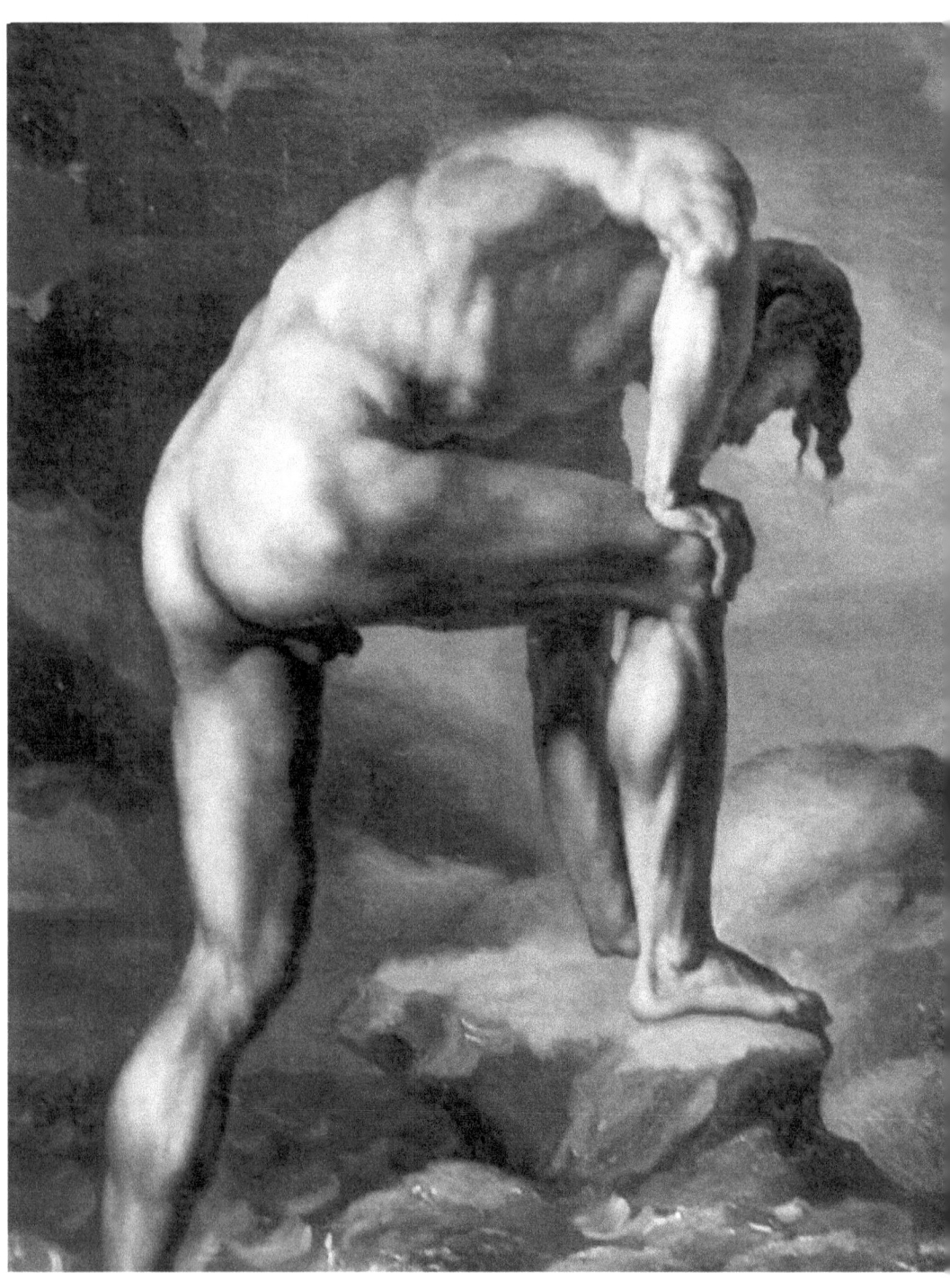

Jean-Louis Andre Theodore Géricault, A Shipwreck, c. 1819

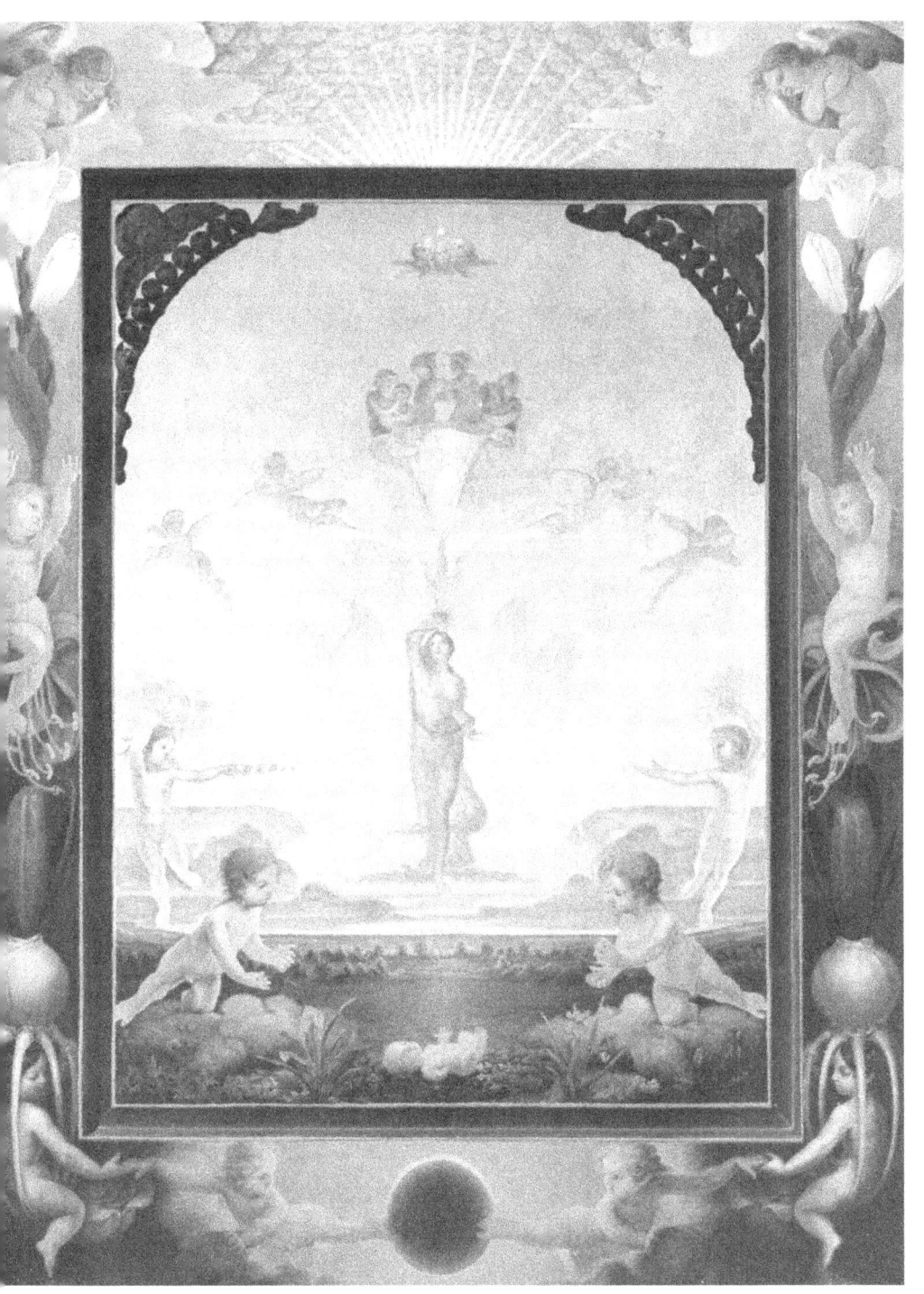

Philipp Otto Runge, Morning, 1808, Hamburg

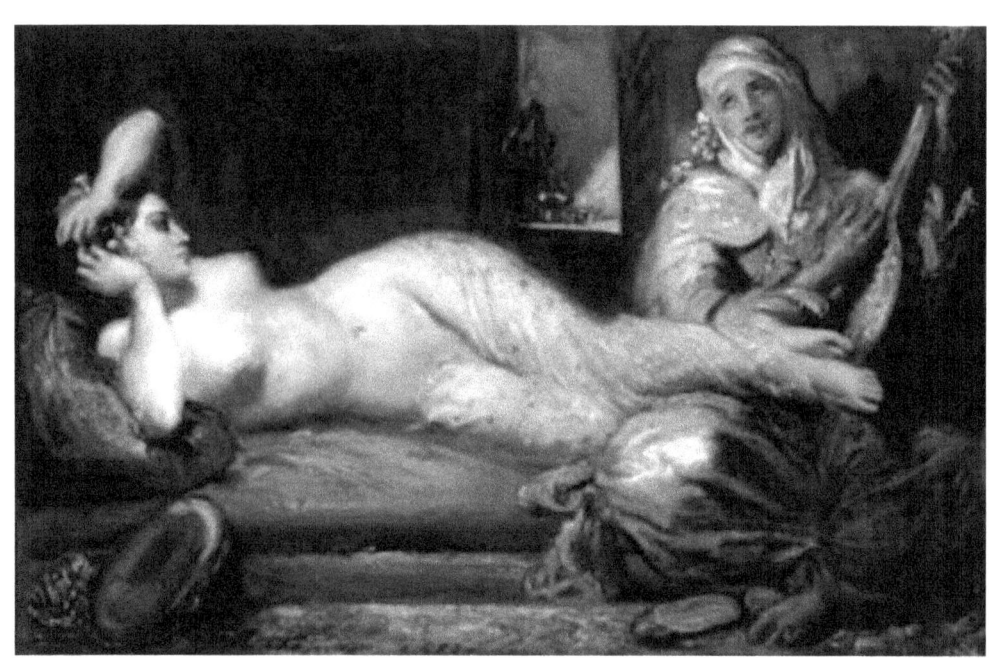

Théodore Chasséreau (1819-56)

J.M.W. Turner, The Blue Rigi, Lake of Lucerne, Sunrise,
1842, Clore Gallery, London

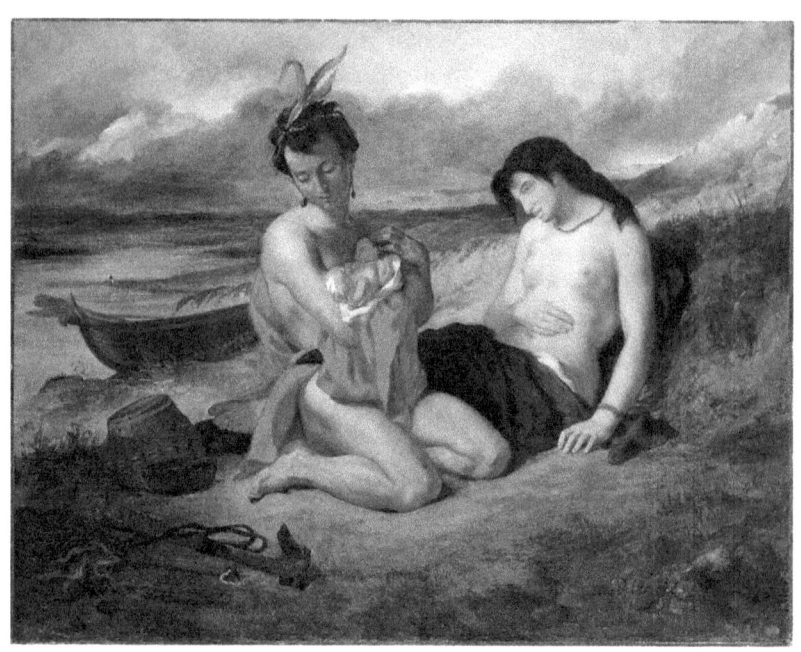

Eugène Delacroix, Les Natchez, 1835, Metropolitan Museum of Art (above).
A Sultan of Morocco, 1862 (below).

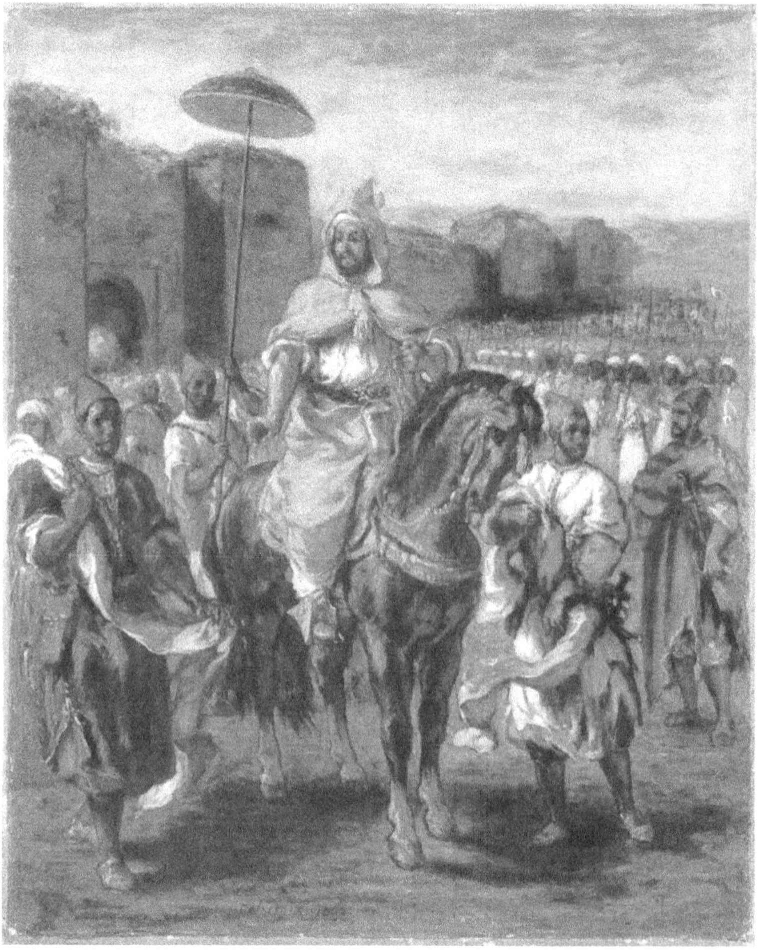

NOTES ON WORKS

FERDINAND GUILLEMARDET
(Museum of the Louvre)

This personage, who has left no record in history, was one of those high functionaries, half civil and half military, whom the First Republic sent to its armies to supervise the commissary department and also to exercise an espionage over its generals. Goya has given a vigorous rendering of a head that bears the double stamp of energy and high breeding; and the prevailing gray tone of this portrait, relieved only by the one dash of brightness in the tricoloured scarf, forms altogether a work of perfect harmony.

LA MAJA (CLOTHED)
(Museum of the Prado, Madrid)

This reclining woman represents a very characteristic type of Spanish beauty. Goya has painted this picture under two different aspects, although in an absolutely identical pose. In one, the woman is represented completely nude, while here the artist has clothed her in corselet and trousers. It is asserted that the Duchess of Alba served him as model for both of these pictures.

THE WOMAN WITH THE FAN
(Museum of the Louvre)

The Louvre is not rich in works by Goya; it possesses only four. But the portrait of a woman, which is here reproduced, belongs to the period of the painter's second manner, in which a most precise realism went hand in hand with a vaporous lightness and a pervading grayness of tone that recalls the most delicate creations of Prudhon. But the execution is vigorous, and in the expression of the face and in the employment of the colours there are a sureness and an intensity that are remarkable.

PORTRAIT OF GOYA
(Museum of the Prado, Madrid)

In this portrait the artist is already old, but his physiognomy has preserved that vivacity of movement, that expression of penetration and irony, which made him such a brilliant figure at the Court of Spain. This work, like every other which bears his signature, is distinguished by the vigour of its execution and beauty of colouring.

THE DUCHESS OF ALBA
(Collection of the Duke of Alba, Madrid)

This superb portrait, the privilege of reproducing which we owe to his Excellence, the Duke of Alba, was painted by Goya with all the confidence of genius, guided by gratitude and friendship. The ties of mutual esteem which united the artist and the duchess are well known, and this portrait in a certain sense constitutes an acknowledgment of it.

This first attempt had the result of enlightening Goya as to his own powers. Not that he had previously mistrusted them, but he had feared that he was not yet sufficiently equipped to venture upon a public appearance. But on the strength of the success of his cartoons he took stock of himself as follows: "He was thirty years of age and he realized now that he had only to take his brush in hand in order to become a great painter."

KING CHARLES IV AND HIS FAMILY
(Museum of the Prado, Madrid)

Goya was the favourite painter of the king Charles IV, who conferred upon him the title of First Painter. In this fine painting, which raised the reputation of the artist to its zenith, the members of the royal family are admirably and sincerely rendered, without a trace of flattery. All the degeneracy of the dynasty is to be read in these countenances, in terms of convincing eloquence.

LA TIRANA
(Museum of the Prado, Madrid)

La Tirana was a famous actress in Madrid during the reign of Charles IV. Goya painted her at the time when he was in the full height of his renown, and celebrities of every kind at the capital quarrelled with one another for the privilege of being painted by him.

JOSEFA BAYEU
(Museum of the Prado, Madrid)

Josefa Bayeu was the sister of the painter Francisco Bayeu, like Goya, a native of Aragon, and his intimate friend. It was in the home of his comrade that Goya fell in love with Josefa and married her. He had one son, Xavier Goya. This portrait is considered as one of the best executed by the artist.

In this work, as in all others by this artist, both the personal and the national note are found to be strongly imprinted; all the participants in this scene are authentic Spaniards, whose classic types may still be recognized to-day in every city throughout the peninsula.

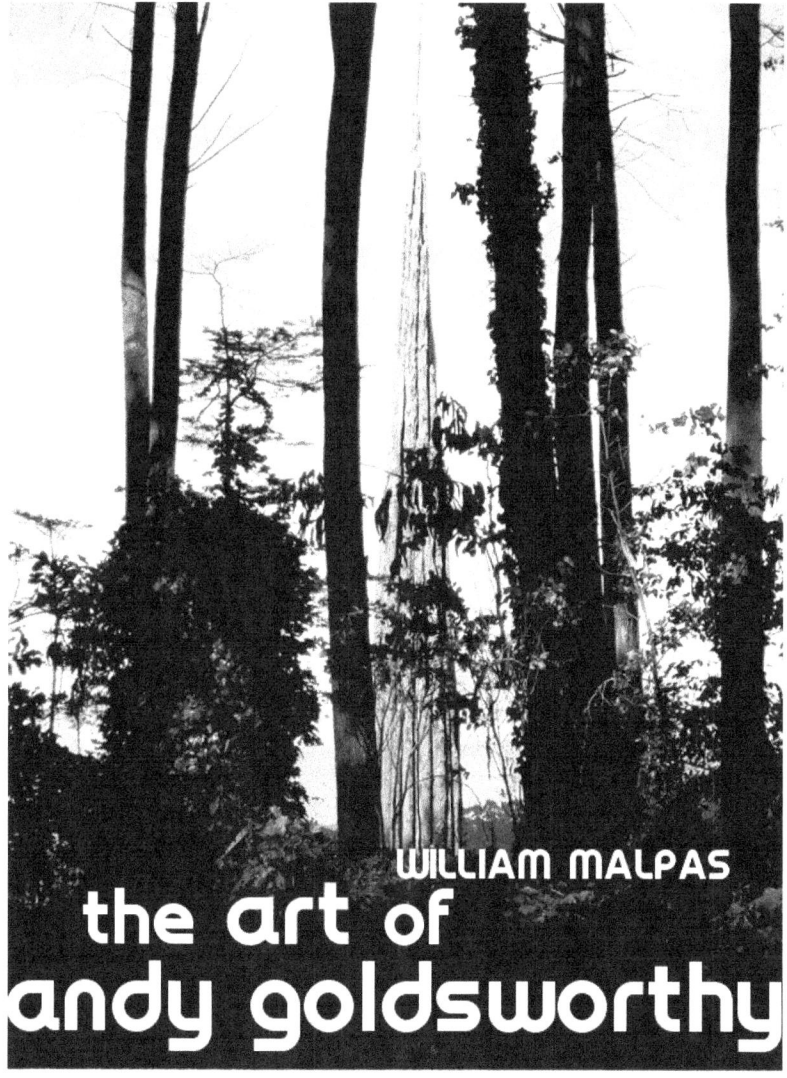

WILLIAM MALPAS
the art of
andy goldsworthy

This is the most comprehensive and detailed account of the art of Andy Goldsworthy available.

This study of Andy Goldsworthy discusses all of Goldsworthy's major exhibitions, books and projects, including the *Sheepfolds* project; *Garden of Stones* in New York; TV and dance collaborations; and the books *Wood, Stone, Time* and *Passage*. William Malpas surveys all of Goldsworthy's output, and analyzes his relation with other land artists such as Robert Smithson, the Christos, Walter de Maria, Chris Drury, Richard Long and David Nash; women sculptors; sculpture in the modern era; and Goldsworthy's place in the contemporary British art scene.

The book has been updated and revised for this new edition.

ISBN 9781861714107 Pbk   ISBN 9781861714114 Hbk
Fully illustrated   www.crmoon.com

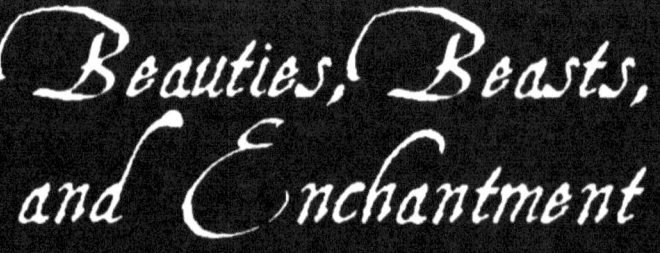

Beauties, Beasts, and Enchantment

CLASSIC FRENCH FAIRY TALES

Translated and with an Introduction
by Jack Zipes

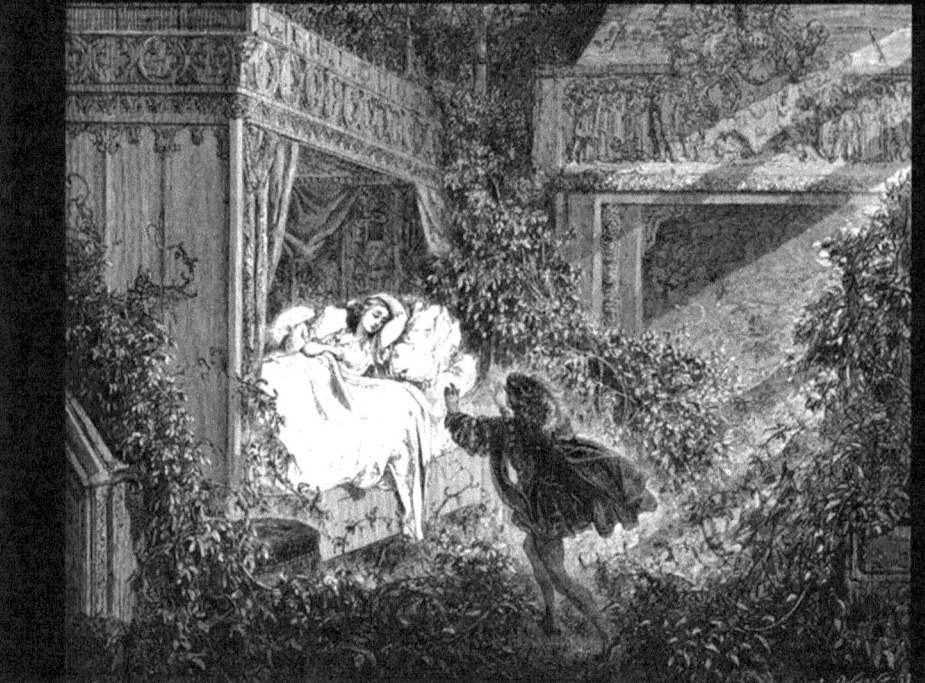

A collection of 36 classic French fairy tales translated by renowned writer Jack Zipes.
Cinderella, Beauty and the Beast, Sleeping Beauty and *Little Red Riding Hood* are among the
classic fairy tales in this amazing book.
Includes illustrations from fairy tale collections.
Jack Zipes has written and published widely on fairy tales.

'Terrific... a succulent array of 17th and 18th century 'salon' fairy tales'
- *The New York Times Book Review*

'These tales are adventurous, thrilling in a way fairy tales are meant to be... The translation
from the French is modern, happily free of archaic and hyperbolic language... a fine and
sophisticated collection' - *New York Tribune*

'Enjoyable to read... a unique collection of French regional folklore' - *Library Journal*

'Charming stories accompanied by attractive pen-and-ink drawings' - *Chattanooga Times*

Introduction and illustrations   612pp.   ISBN 9781861712510 Pbk   ISBN 9781861713193 Hbk

MAURICE SENDAK

& the art of children's book illustration

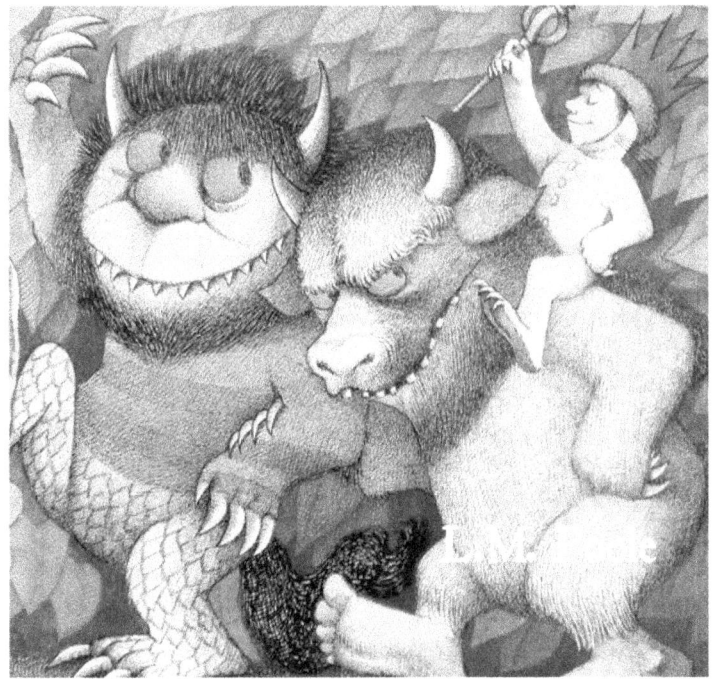

Maurice Sendak is the widely acclaimed American children's book author and illustrator. This critical study focuses on his famous trilogy, *Where the Wild Things Are, In the Night Kitchen* and *Outside Over There*, as well as the early works and Sendak's superb depictions of the Grimm Brothers' fairy tales in *The Juniper Tree*. L.M. Poole begins with a chapter on children's book illustration, in particular the treatment of fairy tales. Sendak's work is situated within the history of children's book illustration, and he is compared with many contemporary authors.

Fully illustrated. The book has been revised and updated for this edition.

ISBN 9781861714282 Pbk   ISBN 9781861713469 Hbk

CRESCENT MOON PUBLISHING

web: www.crmoon.com e-mail: cresmopub@yahoo.co.uk

ARTS, PAINTING, SCULPTURE

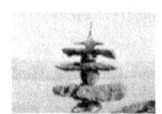
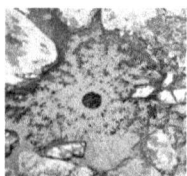

The Art of Andy Goldsworthy
Andy Goldsworthy: Touching Nature
Andy Goldsworthy in Close-Up
Andy Goldsworthy: Pocket Guide
Andy Goldsworthy In America
Land Art: A Complete Guide
The Art of Richard Long
Richard Long: Pocket Guide
Land Art In the UK
Land Art in Close-Up
Land Art In the U.S.A.
Land Art: Pocket Guide
Installation Art in Close-Up
Minimal Art and Artists In the 1960s and After
Colourfield Painting
Land Art DVD, TV documentary
Andy Goldsworthy DVD, TV documentary
The Erotic Object: Sexuality in Sculpture From Prehistory to the Present Day
Sex in Art: Pornography and Pleasure in Painting and Sculpture
Postwar Art
Sacred Gardens: The Garden in Myth, Religion and Art
Glorification: Religious Abstraction in Renaissance and 20th Century Art
Early Netherlandish Painting
Leonardo da Vinci
Piero della Francesca
Giovanni Bellini
Fra Angelico: Art and Religion in the Renaissance
Mark Rothko: The Art of Transcendence
Frank Stella: American Abstract Artist
Jasper Johns
Brice Marden
Alison Wilding: The Embrace of Sculpture
Vincent van Gogh: Visionary Landscapes
Eric Gill: Nuptials of God
Constantin Brancusi: Sculpting the Essence of Things
Max Beckmann
Caravaggio
Gustave Moreau
Egon Schiele: Sex and Death In Purple Stockings
Delizioso Fotografico Fervore: Works In Process 1
Sacro Cuore: Works In Process 2
The Light Eternal: J.M.W. Turner
The Madonna Glorified: Karen Arthurs

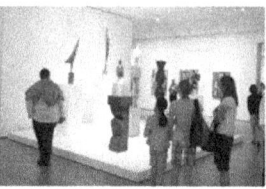
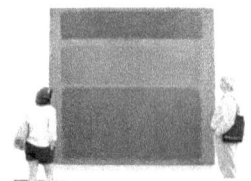
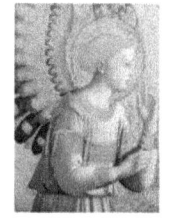
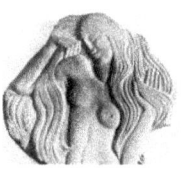
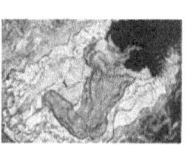
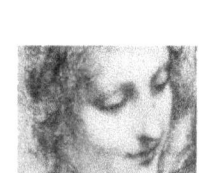
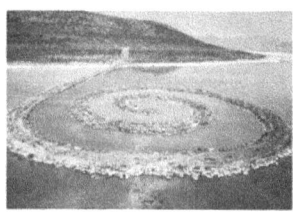

LITERATURE

J.R.R. Tolkien: The Books, The Films, The Whole Cultural Phenomenon
J.R.R. Tolkien: Pocket Guide
Tolkien's Heroic Quest
The *Earthsea* Books of Ursula Le Guin
Beauties, Beasts and Enchantment: Classic French Fairy Tales
German Popular Stories by the Brothers Grimm
Philip Pullman and *His Dark Materials*
Sexing Hardy: Thomas Hardy and Feminism
Thomas Hardy's *Tess of the d'Urbervilles*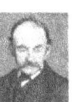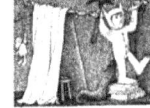
Thomas Hardy's *Jude the Obscure*
Thomas Hardy: The Tragic Novels
Love and Tragedy: Thomas Hardy
The Poetry of Landscape in Hardy
Wessex Revisited: Thomas Hardy and John Cowper Powys
Wolfgang Iser: Essays and Interviews
Petrarch, Dante and the Troubadours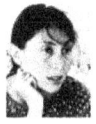
Maurice Sendak and the Art of Children's Book Illustration
Andrea Dworkin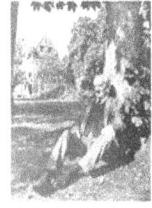
Cixous, Irigaray, Kristeva: The *Jouissance* of French Feminism
Julia Kristeva: Art, Love, Melancholy, Philosophy, Semiotics and Psychoanalysis
Hélène Cixous I Love You: The *Jouissance* of Writing
Luce Irigaray: Lips, Kissing, and the Politics of Sexual Difference
Peter Redgrove: Here Comes the Flood
Peter Redgrove: Sex-Magic-Poetry-Cornwall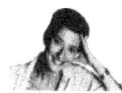
Lawrence Durrell: Between Love and Death, East and West
Love, Culture & Poetry: Lawrence Durrell
Cavafy: Anatomy of a Soul
German Romantic Poetry: Goethe, Novalis, Heine, Hölderlin
Feminism and Shakespeare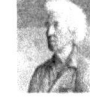
Shakespeare: Love, Poetry & Magic
The Passion of D.H. Lawrence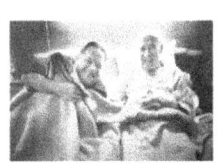
D.H. Lawrence: Symbolic Landscapes
D.H. Lawrence: Infinite Sensual Violence
Rimbaud: Arthur Rimbaud and the Magic of Poetry
The Ecstasies of John Cowper Powys
Sensualism and Mythology: The Wessex Novels of John Cowper Powys
Amorous Life: John Cowper Powys and the Manifestation of Affectivity (H.W. Fawkner)
Postmodern Powys: New Essays on John Cowper Powys (Joe Boulter)
Rethinking Powys: Critical Essays on John Cowper Powys
Paul Bowles & Bernardo Bertolucci
Rainer Maria Rilke
Joseph Conrad: *Heart of Darkness*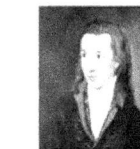
In the Dim Void: Samuel Beckett
Samuel Beckett Goes into the Silence
André Gide: Fiction and Fervour
Jackie Collins and the Blockbuster Novel
Blinded By Her Light: The Love-Poetry of Robert Graves
The Passion of Colours: Travels In Mediterranean Lands
Poetic Forms

POETRY

Ursula Le Guin: Walking In Cornwall
Peter Redgrove: Here Comes The Flood
Peter Redgrove: Sex-Magic-Poetry-Cornwall
Dante: Selections From the Vita Nuova
Petrarch, Dante and the Troubadours
William Shakespeare: Sonnets
William Shakespeare: Complete Poems
Blinded By Her Light: The Love-Poetry of Robert Graves
Emily Dickinson: Selected Poems
Emily Brontë: Poems
Thomas Hardy: Selected Poems
Percy Bysshe Shelley: Poems
John Keats: Selected Poems
Joh n Keats: Poems of 1820
D.H. Lawrence: Selected Poems
Edmund Spenser: Poems
Edmund Spenser: Amoretti
John Donne: Poems
Henry Vaughan: Poems
Sir Thomas Wyatt: Poems
Robert Herrick: Selected Poems
Rilke: Space, Essence and Angels in the Poetry of Rainer Maria Rilke
Rainer Maria Rilke: Selected Poems
Friedrich Hölderlin: Selected Poems
Arseny Tarkovsky: Selected Poems
Arthur Rimbaud: Selected Poems
Arthur Rimbaud: A Season in Hell
Arthur Rimbaud and the Magic of Poetry
Novalis: Hymns To the Night
German Romantic Poetry
Paul Verlaine: Selected Poems
Elizaethan Sonnet Cycles
D.J. Enright: By-Blows
Jeremy Reed: Brigitte's Blue Heart
Jeremy Reed: Claudia Schiffer's Red Shoes
Gorgeous Little Orpheus
Radiance: New Poems
Crescent Moon Book of Nature Poetry
Crescent Moon Book of Love Poetry
Crescent Moon Book of Mystical Poetry
Crescent Moon Book of Elizabethan Love Poetry
Crescent Moon Book of Metaphysical Poetry
Crescent Moon Book of Romantic Poetry
Pagan America: New American Poetry

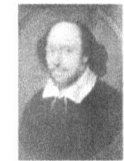
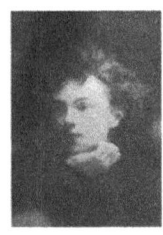
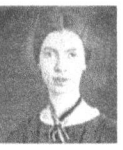
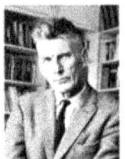
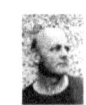
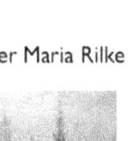
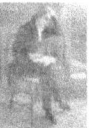
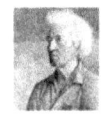
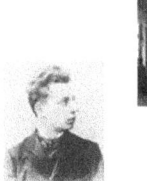
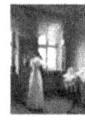
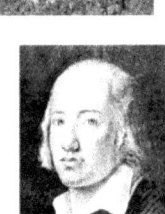
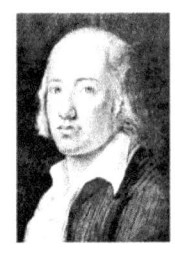

MEDIA, CINEMA, FEMINISM and CULTURAL STUDIES

J.R.R. Tolkien: The Books, The Films, The Whole Cultural Phenomenon
J.R.R. Tolkien: Pocket Guide
The *Lord of the Rings* Movies: Pocket Guide
The Cinema of Hayao Miyazaki
Hayao Miyazaki: *Princess Mononoke*: Pocket Movie Guide
Hayao Miyazaki: *Spirited Away*: Pocket Movie Guide
Tim Burton : Hallowe'en For Hollywood
Ken Russell
Ken Russell: *Tommy*: Pocket Movie Guide
The Ghost Dance: The Origins of Religion
The Peyote Cult

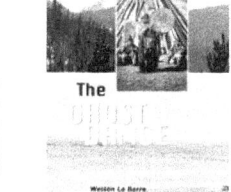
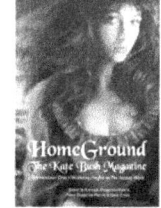

The GHOST DANCE

Cixous, Irigaray, Kristeva: The *Jouissance* of French Feminism
Julia Kristeva: Art, Love, Melancholy, Philosophy, Semiotics and Psychoanalysis
Luce Irigaray: Lips, Kissing, and the Politics of Sexual Difference
Hélene Cixous I Love You: The *Jouissance* of Writing
Andrea Dworkin
'Cosmo Woman': The World of Women's Magazines
Women in Pop Music
HomeGround: The Kate Bush Anthology
Discovering the Goddess (Geoffrey Ashe)
The Poetry of Cinema
The Sacred Cinema of Andrei Tarkovsky
Andrei Tarkovsky: Pocket Guide
Andrei Tarkovsky: *Mirror*: Pocket Movie Guide
Andrei Tarkovsky: *The Sacrifice*: Pocket Movie Guide
Walerian Borowczyk: Cinema of Erotic Dreams
Jean-Luc Godard: The Passion of Cinema
Jean-Luc Godard: *Hail Mary*: Pocket Movie Guide
Jean-Luc Godard: *Contempt*: Pocket Movie Guide
Jean-Luc Godard: *Pierrot le Fou*: Pocket Movie Guide
John Hughes and Eighties Cinema
Ferris Bueller's Day Off: Pocket Movie Guide
Jean-Luc Godard: Pocket Guide
The Cinema of Richard Linklater
Liv Tyler: Star In Ascendance
Blade Runner and the Films of Philip K. Dick
Paul Bowles and Bernardo Bertolucci
Media Hell: Radio, TV and the Press
An Open Letter to the BBC
Detonation Britain: Nuclear War in the UK
Feminism and Shakespeare
Wild Zones: Pornography, Art and Feminism
Sex in Art: Pornography and Pleasure in Painting and Sculpture
Sexing Hardy: Thomas Hardy and Feminism

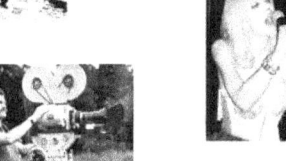
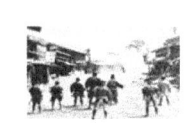
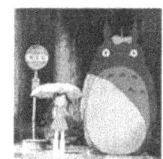
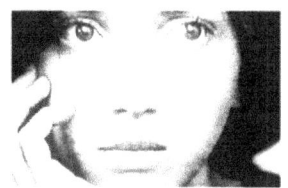

HomeGround
The Kate Bush Magazine

The Light Eternal is a model monograph, an exemplary job. The subject matter of the book is beautifully
organised and dead on beam. (Lawrence Durrell)
It is amazing for me to see my work treated with such passion and respect. (Andrea Dworkin)

CRESCENT MOON PUBLISHING
P.O. Box 1312, Maidstone, Kent, ME14 5XU, Great Britain. www.crmoon.com

cresmopub@yahoo.co.uk   www.crescentmoon.org.uk

www.ingramcontent.com/pod-product-compliance
Lightning Source LLC
Chambersburg PA
CBHW051326220526

45468CB00004B/1522

9 781861 716248